Memoir of a Sceptical Seeker

TESSA HILLMAN

Published by Top of the Village Publishing 2023

topofthevillagepublishing.co.uk

Text copyright © 2023 Tessa Hillman
Illustrations copyright © 2023 Tessa Hillman

Tessa Hillman asserts her moral right to be identified as the author of this work. All rights reserved. No part of this publication may be reproduced in any form or by any means without the prior permission of the author.
Contact: tessa.hillman2@gmail.com

Website: yogastories.co.uk
Illustration: Tessa Hillman
Cover design: Alan Nisbet, Liz Hyde
ISBN paperback: 978-1-7399846-4-9
ISBN ebook: 978-1-7399846-5-6

Tessa Hillman August 2023

Contents

Timeline		10
Foreword		15

CHAPTERS	SUBJECTS	
Chapter 1 Introduction		17
Part One Chapter 2 This is My Story	Berrio; Healing day; Mrs Joyce	22
Chapter 3 The Green Aura From 'sinner' to seeker to healer	Primary teaching; keep-fit; healing course; healing practice	32
Chapter 4 Hot Coals and Other Hot Things Looking back at Earth-bound early married life, and on to 'mystical' middle age	Peru; fairy friends; Cornish cottage; fire walk	41

Chapter 5 Zambia A shocking event that made me wonder about angelic rescues	PGCE; Gerry arrives; the attack	49
Chapter 6 The Ouija Board A dangerous adventure which opened a door that should have stayed shut	A teenage experience	55
Chapter 7 *Meditation Circles* The path to enlightenment started here in a strange and captivating way	First circle; guardian angel; meet Guptananda; first story; Calling Horse; Niasco; channelling	59
Chapter 8 *Healing Body, Mind and spirit – Mine and Others* Some dramatic happenings during healing sessions	Chakras and the pendulum; past lives; angelic encounter	71

Chapter 9 ***More About The Healing Course at Unity House, Plymouth*** Healing becomes a reality	Protection and grounding; closing down	80
Chapter 10 ***Writing Stories for Other People*** The Babel Fish enters my ear	Psychic artist; educational stories; Babel fish; guidance for sons	86
Chapter 11 ***On-screen Spiritual Happenings*** Publishing the book and blog online	My book online; the blog; a message on my computer screen	99
Chapter 12 ***The Flood*** One of my favourite channelled stories, written for a worldwide educational scheme	A lovely story illustrating respecting other peoples' property – or 'non-stealing'	104

Chapter 13 **Sound Mantra** A simple sound leads to a wonderful, uplifting message that keeps me positive for years	A meditation technique	111
Chapter 14 **The End of an Era** We leave our country cottage	Things fall apart, but change for the better	114
Chapter 15 **Teaching in the College of Further Education** Dreams, energy zaps and visual things	My new job; several strange spiritual happenings	120
Chapter 16 **Psychometry and Visions** Starting my own meditation group at home	Meditating on objects; significant visions; crystal healing; Bryn's spirit	127
Chapter 17 **Quan Yin** A goddess comes into my life, unbidden, bringing comfort and help	A goddess arrives; we make statues; my brother's illness;	138

| Chapter 18
Guidance and messages for others	Spirits come to bring messages	145
Chapter 19
Conclusion
A science teacher's way of saying, 'The end, and I hope you got something out of it' | | 151 |
| Part Two
A Background to My Childhood
Putting this book into perspective | My Polish father – from 'hero to zero' and back again | 154 |

| Appendix 1
The subtle energy system		173
Appendix 2
The workings of a pendulum		177
Acknowledgements		185

Timeline

This will be useful if you want to know the chronological order of events

Year	My Age	Life situation	Spiritual happenings
1950	0–7	Farm Life Exmoor	Fairies
1953	3	Brother P born	
1957-1968	7–18	Town life in Ipswich	
1959	9	'Baby' brother born	
1964	14	Grammar school	Ouija board
1968-1972	18–21	Nottingham University	
1971	21–22	Zambia Married Gerry	Attacked; saved
1974	24	First son born in Nottingham	
1977	25–27	Peru	

Year	My Age	Life situation	Spiritual happenings
1976	26	Teaching Yoga	
1977	27	Second son born in Peru	
1978	28–53	Cornish cottage	
1985	32–35	Yoga Teaching diploma	
1993–2023	43–72	Spiritual events began	Healing and mediums' revelations; dowsing; channelling; past life experiences; mediumship experiences
1995	45–51	Healing Course in Plymouth	
1997–2002	47–52	CPCAB (Courses in Counselling Skills and Therapeutic Counselling)	

Year	My Age	Life situation	Spiritual happenings
2003	53–64	Left G. Moved to a town. Started new teaching career at FE college	Worked at Bodmin mental hospital and Duchy College
2008	58	Married Bryn	
2008	58	Published online book, *'Guptananda's Stories'*	
2010	60	Bryn died Sept	Energy zaps started in April
2011	61	Met David	
2014	63	Married David. Country life again	
2014	64	Retired	
2015	64–65	Returned to Unity House, Plymouth, to teach healing course for a year	First visions of people's guides

Year	My Age	Life situation	Spiritual happenings
2015	65		Quan Yin appeared; Other visions
2016	66	Started own meditation circle at home	Psychometry brings proof of other realms
2019	69	Published Book 1 paperback and ebook Stories taken from online book 'Guptananda's Stories'	
2020	70	Covid pandemic 2020 -2022	Mother Earth picture vision and painting
2021	71	Completed Book 2, 'Yoga Stories from Guru Guptananda'	

Year	My Age	Life situation	Spiritual happenings
2021	71	Wrote my memoir, this book. Created Top of the Village Publishing	Saw a spirit/ghost in my bedroom, and astral body of our dog – a first
2022	72	Published Book 2	Spirit Visitation from Bryn

Foreword

This book is more than a memoir, it's a detailing of one self-confessed sceptic's gradual awareness of a deeper, wider, brighter, and all-enveloping world. It's an invitation to explore that world through personal experiences, to accept or discard elements of those experiences as you go, and to take any comfort you might find within these pages. That comfort is yours to keep, and given freely.

The stories in this book are as varied and startling as anything you are likely to read or hear anywhere in the world; revelations from the heart of the Cornish moors, for instance, that wouldn't sound out of place had they appeared scorched into stone on some Himalayan mountaintop. They are written with the kind of humility and honesty that breathes truth into every word.

The author posits that spiritual help exists beyond what we see and hear every day in the normal course of a busy life, and that, if we know how to search for that help, we can find many of the answers we're seeking – though not always in the ways we might expect. You will learn some of the ways the author has interpreted her own lived experiences, and, with the wealth of the information given, you can learn to do the same.

You will find no preaching in this book, nor any arguments as to the validity, or otherwise, of any recognisable religion; instead you will find stories to enthrall, to both feed and satisfy your curiosity, or simply to absorb and enjoy.

Terri Nixon

Terri Nixon, well established and successful author of over 15 books of historical fiction, born in the West Country, and deeply rooted in Cornwall offered this preface to me after reading my memoir. Thank you so much Terri, you have recognised in my book some deep and important truths that I have hoped to convey.

~ CHAPTER 1 ~

Introduction

Have you ever wondered if there is anything beyond this world where we live and experience our struggles and triumphs? Most people do. After death, do we just turn to dust and ashes, or is there an existence beyond death? It was a major preoccupation for me, and for the first forty-three years of my life I found little in the way of answers. This book shows how as a sceptical 'scientist' – a biology teacher with a degree in botany – I was driven to accept that scientific logic failed to explain the experiences that I had been having, and how I came to discover a new logic. It wasn't a logic that can be defined and described, or proved to others. Only through experience can we reach that stage of understanding. It is often easier for people to turn their backs on the inexplicable, shrug their shoulders and move uncritically on. But the spiritual search and journey have been of huge value to me, and I would recommend a willingness to be open to 'something else' as you read these pages. Will you come with me?

I want to write about my life through the lens of my experiences that led me from being a non-believer, disillusioned with 'the church' (with a crack of hope that there was something bigger than this life), to a totally convinced believer in other realms. These realms remain hard to define, but I have glimpsed enough of them to have found a great comfort and solace in my life. Quite where and what 'God' is, and how they/he/she fits into the picture is still a puzzle, but I feel it is well worthwhile praying and being open to help and guidance.

I have never been able to believe anything that was not proven beyond doubt to me. This book tells the story of my 'proofs' and other incidents – I call them proofs because they have convinced me. My hope is that it may encourage others to keep searching and investigating until certainty happens for them. We are living through a very difficult time right now. We have emerged from the Covid pandemic, but climate change is already happening and faster than was ever anticipated, and we are currently witnessing a terrible war in the Ukraine, Palestine and Israel, and on-going wars in Africa. If we were open to the help that is available, I believe that life would not be nearly as traumatic and problematic. If you already have a faith that does not condemn all others who don't share it, and your faith includes a non-judgemental god, or overarching Higher Power, then you are lucky. If you do not hold those kinds of beliefs, you will see that there are other ways of approaching this vital matter. It does seem to be *vital* to me. See what you make of my experiences, they may ring true to you too.

I have changed the names of some people in my story to protect their privacy.

My accounts are not all in chronological order. It makes more sense to me to present them as I have done, because I have grouped together similar events, and these might stretch over many decades. Use the **Timeline** that is shown after the **Contents Table** to help you navigate the happenings in the chapters, if you need to.

~ PART ONE ~

~ CHAPTER 2 ~

This is My Story

This is my story and I need to travel forwards and backwards in time to show you the whole picture. Life changed for me when I was forty-three, and had no spiritual beliefs at all. Then a series of spiritually eye-opening events occurred. At one point I did not sleep for three days, because I was so excited and thrilled to know at last that 'the other side' existed.

On the face of it, life in my early forties was good. I was teaching my yoga classes and training to teach keep-fit. The smallholding that we had set up fifteen years previously kept me happily busy. My husband Gerry and I had read John Seymour's crazily optimistic and unrealistic, *The Complete Book of Self-Sufficiency,* and were inspired. We reared chickens and ducks, and we fenced off the corner of our field and turned it into a veg garden. It was fun to experiment with growing every kind of vegetable we could think of. We had dug out a sloping field next to our house, terraced it and planted out a beautiful garden that we designed round the house and stream. Gerry – often called G by me – did a lot of the donkey work, barrowing soil from one place to another, collecting and moving heavy stones to create a rustic henhouse and a secret garden. I joined in and did as much as I could – there was the day I loaded and pushed eleven full barrows of soil to create a flat area where our two sons could play ball games, before my arms refused to work any more! No more digging, lifting soil or barrowing was possible for me that day, but there seemed to be no limit to the amount of work that G could do. I decided I was better suited to chatting to the neighbours about gardening and cadging plants to populate our large new garden.

G, a landscape painter, was doing well. He held exhibitions every two years, on which we depended for an income. However, in spite of my great happiness, something was missing in my life, something important, though I didn't really know what it was. My yoga training had suggested that spiritual understanding is the inevitable outcome of practising yoga, but I had no sense whatever of the 'spiritual side of life' yet it was something I truly wanted. I thought of joining a church, or going to pagan circles or visiting an ashram. However none of these activities appealed. In fact I was afraid of them. I didn't want to get drawn in to organisations where people would be telling me of the consequences I might suffer if I did or didn't do this or that. As a child, that had been my experience of the Catholic Church. I didn't want to have to answer to vicars or priests, and I wasn't impressed by our sleazy choirmaster who'd put his hand on my knee and told me that his wife (and mother of his six kids) didn't love him.

I used to go to confession on Saturday mornings, but perhaps only when I thought I had accumulated enough sins for it to be worth the ten-minute walk down to St Mary's Church, at the end of our road. When I was about twelve, I was led into doing something that I was embarrassed about. I did not go to confession that Saturday. On the Sunday I took holy communion at the altar. The following Saturday I felt brave enough to go to confession. I confessed my sins to the priest as we sat in the private confessional box, he and I separated by a curtain and a wooden partition. He told me that because I had taken communion (eaten a wafer of bread, representing the body of Christ) while in a state of sin, I had now committed a ***mortal sin***. Had I been run over by a bus at that point, I would have gone straight to hell. Not his words exactly, but I have to make light of it because back then I thought it was both tosh and terrifying at the same time! The punishment for missing Sunday mass was just the same. Hell and damnation! As if a 'loving god' would do that to a child of twelve who was led into making a stupid mistake. It wasn't long before I left the church. I am aware that my Catholic upbringing contributed a great deal to my sense of right and wrong, and I am grateful for that.

Back to me at 43 years of age…Among our circle of friends there was one person whom I particularly admired. She seemed to be very worldly-wise. She was a school teacher and a masseuse. She used to come to my yoga classes and invited me to a 'healing day', in the old mine captain's house in Minions, up on Bodmin Moor, about a mile from where we lived. A 'healing day'! I had always avoided such things. They were far too 'woo-woo' for me; or so I thought. However, overtaken by curiosity and intrigue, I decided to go. I took the precaution of going with a trusted friend.

It was summer, the moor was glorious and I was with my best friend. I was feeling full of joy and energy, and I entered the mine captain's house excitedly, hoping for some kind of revelation. I was vaguely aware of chakras, or energy centres, because we paid lip service to them in yoga. Those in the know explained that the practice of yoga opens the energy centres in the body and allows old traumatic and problematic energy to flow out (and I certainly had a bit of that, as you will see). New, vital healing energy could then flow in. Many yoga teachers believe that it is not usually necessary to go to a counsellor to sort out one's 'issues'. Yoga asanas (exercises), breathing practises and meditation should normally suffice. I had discovered that through yoga breathing practice and visualisation, I could energise my solar plexus, one of the main energy centres, and actually raise the temperature of that area. This made me feel really good, both physically and mentally.

I arrived at the mine captain's house to be greeted by a pleasant, confident woman called Anna. She offered to measure my chakras with a pendulum and to give me healing. This was a totally new concept to me and, as I was feeling bold and curious, I accepted her offer.

"I don't often see chakras in such a good healthy state," she told me. "What do you do that makes you so well balanced?"

"I do teach yoga and keep-fit, and practice every day at home, oh, and I meditate a lot too. Would that be the reason?" I asked.

"Oh, very likely," she answered. "The chakras reflect our life's experience, our attitudes and our traumas. You do have one chakra that is showing signs of a problem. It's your sacral chakra."

Immediately I knew what the cause of that might be. It was there at my belly that her pendulum had suddenly started to move in a different way. The sacral chakra is known to be the centre of sexual and creative energy. She asked me if I had experienced any trauma in that area. I certainly had.

At twenty-two years old, I had been attacked and raped while I was on VSO (Voluntary Service Overseas) in Africa. It was an event that caused me to become very fearful for my life whenever I was alone in the countryside, (and which still affects me even now as I enter my eighth decade). This seemed to me to be a likely cause of my damaged sacral energy centre. I was fascinated by what Anna told me during my healing session with her and impressed by the accuracy of her diagnosis. She gave me hope that I could be healed. She said that, because my other chakras were in such a good, open and active state, I myself could become a healer, if I corrected the damaged one – the sacral chakra. 'Healing' was totally beyond anything that I had ever experienced, but I did think it would be worth considering getting myself 'fixed', hopefully to become more of a 'whole' human being. Two of my own yoga class members were healers whom I knew could be trusted to try to help me.

Right at the very end of the session, Anna mentioned that someone from the spirit world called Joyce wanted to speak to me. I couldn't think of any friend or relative, dead or alive, called Joyce, so I just said that I didn't know anyone by that name, and let it go at that. Much to my surprise, however, 'Joyce' was soon to re-enter my life in a way I would never have imagined possible. This was the turning point in my life, though I didn't recognise it at the time

That day of healing started me off on a lifetime's exploration. Some of my friends also became interested in this line of investigation and the four of us, including my husband, ventured into a spiritualist church in the nearby town. I must admit I was a bit nervous. The Catholic Church certainly would not have approved, and I was still following their rules as set out in the Ten Commandments. However, I felt that their edicts that one must not attend any religious events other than Catholic ones were more about holding on to their power over people than instilling good behaviour. It was reassuring to be in the company of good friends, and I felt safe in the unusual situation of being in a church filled with people presided over by a professional medium, who had come down to Cornwall from London for the event.

I was reassured by the sign on the door that read 'Christian Spiritualist Church'. It wasn't as if we were doing anything 'outlandish' such as attending a séance, for example. The medium was a sweet lady of Jamaican origin and of about seventy-five years of age. She used a wand with multi-coloured ribbons to help connect with the spirit world. Then, from among these ribbons, she chose one of a particular colour. The ribbon would give her some sort of connection with a person in the congregation, and she would then give them a reading, or a message from 'Spirit'. It was to my husband, G, that she turned first; not to me. What a disappointment – I thought my chances of receiving a reading were now very slim!

She began Gerry's reading, "Your workload will be rapidly increasing. I see a wheelbarrow full of papers; there will be so many sheets that you will need wheels to move them around," she declared.

"I've just been elected to serve on Cornwall County Council!" G announced to the whole hall.

"No, no, don't tell me anything!" Titters and smiles went round the room. I felt a jolt of apprehension when she then turned to me.

"I see a ballet dancer, is that you?"

"I teach yoga," I replied. I could understand how

she might have mistaken yoga for ballet.

"Graceful," she said. Then she told me that somebody called Joyce wanted to speak to me. Joyce! There she was for a second time. I felt the hairs on the back of my head stand up. I repeated what I had said in the mine captain's house: "I don't know anyone called Joyce." Again, that turning point was reaffirmed…

'Well," the medium replied, "she's here and she says she knows you!"

That revelation set me searching back over my life. I couldn't immediately recall anybody I knew who had died, and certainly not anyone called Joyce. It was then that I remembered; I had known not a 'Joyce', but a 'Mrs Joyce'. She was an elderly lady I used to visit and help on a Saturday morning. My friend Pat and I had taken it in turns to see Mrs Joyce. Pat and I were both fifteen, and completing a social services award on our way to earning a stripe as non-commissioned officers in the Girls Venture Corps (the young people's branch of the RAF). For social service duty, we had to visit and help an elderly person for a minimum of six weeks. We used to bring in the coal, make up the fire and enjoy a cup of tea and a chat. How could I leave lonely Mrs Joyce to her own devices after the six weeks were up? I continued to help her until I started my 'A' Level studies. While chatting with her one time, I discovered that she had not seen her family for twenty years. I decided to help reunite them. Somehow, I persuaded the Women's Royal Voluntary

Service to provide a car and driver to take Mrs Joyce and me to London. The driver dropped Mrs Joyce at her family's house where she spent a wonderful day with them, and I was taken to Kew Gardens, where I spent the day admiring the flowers.

Now, here was Mrs Joyce again; I guessed she had come back to say thank you from the world beyond this one! After that I tried to make contact with her in my meditations. I had the impression that she had returned not only to thank me, but also to advise me on my cookery skills, which at the time were sadly lacking. She had spent her working life as the main cook in a 'big house'. Even now, I call on Mrs Joyce when faced with perhaps half a manky cauliflower, three carrots, an onion and some spices. I have created so many truly delicious dishes – all of them unrepeatable, as I can never quite remember the ingredients – and I'm sure Mrs Joyce had something to do with these little successes! I am lucky enough never to be at a loss as to what to cook. I never buy takeaways and never waste any leftovers. Thank you, Mrs Joyce! Many blessings!

So, as I discovered, there is a world of spirits out there and, yes, they can communicate with us in a telepathic way. They do not use normal speech, and to and fro conversations have never been my experience. They do indeed watch over us. However, I am convinced it is unwise to spend too much time trying to communicate with the dead. They may whisper good advice to us in our dreams and meditations, but we have our own lives to live and our own lessons to learn. And we shouldn't forget what my teacher told me – if those now in spirit were not particularly wise when they were alive, then they are not likely to have become saints or all-knowing just because they have passed on. That's the general consensus of opinion anyway, and one that I'll go along with!

~ CHAPTER 3 ~

The Green Aura

From 'sinner' to seeker to healer

Let's go back in time to explain the next step in my spiritual path. With both our boys at school, in my mid-thirties, I had returned to teaching. I tried my hand at working with primary-level children, though I had trained to teach only in secondary school. After a couple of years of full-time voluntary work in classrooms, picking up as many tips as possible, I applied for a part-time job at a small, three-class school in a village on Bodmin Moor. The head had told me that he would take care of the maths and English and I could teach science and anything else I wanted! The children in my class ranged from nine to eleven years old.

I used to cycle six miles to school on fine weather days. It was a hard push uphill of forty-five minutes – then at the end of the day I would glide downhill – home in an easy thirty minutes. I adored the sunshine and the flower-filled lanes. In January there were snowdrops, in February and March came the celandines and primroses, followed by bluebells in April and May and campions then foxgloves in June.

All so typical of the Cornish countryside. I loved those journeys! The preparations for lessons took up much of my time at home. Every lesson had to be worked up from nothing. I was often busy until midnight. My husband found it difficult and so did I. I felt I needed a career, and to be able to add to the family income. It was a mixture of a great challenge and hard work, but also the joy and fun of being with kids and the satisfaction that came with passing my knowledge on to them.

It was all guesswork too. What did they need to know? What were they capable of achieving at their age? I had little or no guidance. In those days a formal school curriculum did not seem to exist. Every single lesson had to be drawn from my life's somewhat rusty memory. After two years of teaching, having taught many of the children for the entire time, I felt I had given them all I knew.

The prospect of finding yet more new material for those who would remain in my class was entirely daunting. There was no internet in those days and the school library was scant and old-fashioned. So, when an *Encyclopaedia Britannica* salesman came to call at our house in a tiny hamlet on Bodmin Moor, he found a ready, if not desperate, customer. I spent my entire year's earnings on the full set of the Encyclopaedias! The books seemed to represent a much wider window on the world than I had at the time. I comforted myself with the thought that it would also provide access to knowledge for our own two boys, now approaching their teens. Sadly, it didn't provide what I needed; it wasn't enough. I decided to stop trying to be a primary school teacher. Without the benefit of primary-level training or a curriculum or materials it was just too darned hard work. I decided I would concentrate on teaching yoga instead.

I had gained a British Wheel of Yoga Teacher's Diploma at thirty-five, in the mid-eighties, and was already a well-established yoga teacher. There was a big demand for my classes, so I increased my teaching from two to four classes per week. I set up in all the local villages at various times and decided to try teaching keep-fit as well. My love of music and dance encouraged me to go down that route, so in my late thirties I thought I should discover what the Keep-Fit Association (KFA) was all about.

I attended lessons for keep-fit teachers – weekend top-ups giving teachers ideas for their own classes. It was wonderful but also very challenging because, although I was very supple and fit, my brain was not used to remembering sequences of movement. In our yoga training we were taught to tackle one pose at a time, paying attention in great detail to the juxtaposition of our limbs. I learnt the importance of relaxing and stretching the various muscles involved in each pose, whilst focusing on the organs in the body that were being toned or affected.

The KFA ladies – keep-fit teachers who came in various shapes and sizes – flowed around the room confidently adding this move to that move, until a whole sequence of at least eight or twelve moves had been tacked together. My graceful body (as one of my yoga students described it) became a stumbling, dithering mess! In my green leotard and tights, emulating the 'Green Goddess' of the TV yoga world, smooth and sleek I may have seemed, but I felt more like a wooden puppet than a ballerina.

'Aerobics', a modern and simplified version of 'keep fit', suddenly became very fashionable in the early nineties. I set up a class based on what Jane Fonda, the celebrity keep fit teacher of the era, was teaching. No need to remember very much, I just went ahead with it. There was a general hunger for aerobics at the time, and I supplied the local demand. The wife of the local headmaster gave me a tape of music suitable for teaching keep-fit moves; so very kind of her. We had no television, so I was totally out of touch with the popular music of the time. She introduced me to Michael Jackson and Prince. What a revelation! I loved those rhythms. The words went over my head, it was the tunes I loved. Many years later I re-listened to some of the songs and it almost makes me blush to think about the words that were issuing from my ghetto blaster into those village halls. Nobody ever took me to one side and asked me if I really ought to be playing such stuff. Perhaps they were all as green as I was and didn't notice either!

I realised I needed to know more about a number of aspects of aerobics so that I could make a better job of the teaching. There was a lot of interest in aerobics at the time, it was a 'new thing', and it was then that our local leisure centre started a course to train aerobics teachers. At last this was something I could train to do properly – repetitive movements, four of each added together, so that we only ever needed to remember a sequence of four moves. Marvellous. No stumbling. I found my milieu. So once I gained my aerobics teacher's certificate, at the age of forty, I then taught two aerobics classes as well as my four yoga classes every week. I was glowingly fit and healthy.

Sitting near the front of my yoga class was Sarah; a lovely, friendly mystical woman with a strong Yorkshire accent. She approached me at the end of one of the yoga sessions.

"Tess, you have a wonderful green aura," she said, "and you should do something with it." I had no idea what she was talking about, but I was intrigued! We arranged to meet up.

This happened at around the same time as my healing experience and the reappearance of Mrs Joyce in my life. Over a cup of tea in her home, Sarah told me about her interest in Spirit, things like the afterlife, reincarnation and God. She told me about her ability to see auras and their significance, and explained that my green aura meant I was a natural healer and that it was a gift I should use – a very fascinating concept for me. I had come across it when I was a primary school pupil, in a little book in the school library. I had been mesmerised by this book, which told tales of healers and healing events. It made a huge impression on me; it gave me a warm glow in my heart. On library days I would rush to the same shelf time after time, hoping to find the book. I remember thinking how wonderful it would be if one could help people to heal, but the book only seemed to refer to people of a past age. It was a world away from what I could aspire to and I let it rest in the memory bank of my childhood days.

Thirty years later I still loved the idea of being a healer and here was Sarah, a second person telling me that I could or even should become one. Anna and Sarah, the two people who had told me this did not know each other and they lived many miles apart.

I still had it in mind when I heard about the Healing Centre in Plymouth, only ten miles away from home. It was summer and they were taking applications for their next healers' training course in the autumn. Three of my friends came to give me moral support at the initial interview. They were curious about what the course had to offer, but I was serious about taking part. I think the lady who interviewed us was a little perplexed by the fact that there were four of us in the tiny interview room. My friends were well behaved if a bit nervous and giggly, and she indulged us. I signed up for the two-year course. It was once a month on a Wednesday evening. I was thrilled to be accepted, if also, being me, slightly sceptical about the whole concept. It gave me a new focus to my life, something I needed and wanted, as I had found I lacked the experience to continue as a primary school teacher. The idea that it could also possibly begin to lift the veil between myself and other realms or levels of existence was wonderfully appealing.

By this time my boys were quite independent and getting ready to leave home, and the empty nest was becoming all too evident. Life had started to lack a sense of fulfilment. The two-year healing course came just at the right moment, promising to be a potential source of great interest and joy, and even a career move if I found that I had a gift for healing.

A few weeks previous to the Plymouth course, Anna, who had measured my energy centres at the mine captain's house, offered a small group of us a day-long course on how to give healing. She and her partner demonstrated the basics of a healing session. She told us that we needed to open ourselves mentally to the highest level we could reach, for example to a deity like Jesus, or Buddha, or to our 'Higher Self'. Anna told us to surround ourselves in Love and Light in order to protect ourselves from any negativity that might be around. She showed us how to use a pendulum to measure people's main chakras. Everyone exists in an energy field, or aura, and the chakras are like vortexes of whirling energy flowing into and out of the body. (More on this in a later chapter). It was an intensive course and I found it all very fascinating.

With these tools I wanted to set about experimentally giving healing or at least sensing energies. But who could I practise on? My husband was a good sport. He had lots of energy and was brimming with good health, so his energy field was likely to be a great example of how a healthy one should feel. In our hamlet we had a few open-minded neighbours. One had nervous problems and the other clearly had health issues, but nothing anyone could pin down. His wife thought I might be able to help him. I describe how his energy field helped me to understand more about the significance of the chakras in a later chapter. The feel of different people's energy fields, or auras, to my hands, surprised me. They could be warm or cold, draughty, electrically buzzy, or exerting a positive pressure, or like a vacuum. They certainly told a tale, though exactly what that tale was I could not yet discern. I read a book called *Hands of Light* to learn more about these energy centres. It was written by Barbara Ann Brennan PhD, an Atmospheric Physicist who had worked for NASA before she entered the world of spiritual healing. I was encouraged to find that someone who was science trained was able to write freely and confidently about a subject that most medical practitioners rejected.

My first 'guinea pig' was the somewhat nervous neighbour of mine. She was feeling apprehensive because her son and daughter-in-law were about to come down from London and their visits always caused her great strain. I used my new-found healing skills hoping to calm her state of mind. As soon as I started, I could feel the edges of her aura and her chakras with my hands. Then I felt some sort of energy exchange taking place. I could feel energy flowing through me and into her. This was such a powerful and, to me, novel experience, that I was moved to tears. I wondered while it was happening if she was gaining any benefit and I was relieved and delighted to hear that she floated happily through the family visit. Later she revealed that her aunt was a healer of considerable repute who had lived to a great age. On reflection, I realised my success on this occasion was down to two aspects of the encounter. My neighbour was open to healing and I was open to giving it.

~ CHAPTER 4 ~

Hot Coals and Other Hot Things

Looking back at Earthbound early married life, and on to 'mystical' middle age

We spent some time living in Peru in the early days of our marriage. Gerry's degree in plant physiology and his background in chemistry, physics and biology made him the perfect candidate for a wonderful job teaching there, in 1976. We were twenty-six and twenty-eight at the time. He was chosen from a huge long list of applicants. Even after the candidates had been whittled down to a short-list, there were still thirty left to choose from. It seemed long odds that he would ever get this plum job. However, the fact that he played the piano and was also a keen and competent sportsman gave him an edge over the rest of the field. The appointing committee considered his versatility would be very useful as he would be able to perform a wide range of duties and teach a variety of different subjects. It had the promise of being a very lucrative job, and we were both thrilled that he had succeeded in securing it.

We moved to Peru with our young son, not quite two years old, and lived on the Altiplano. It is the most extensive area of high plateau on Earth, outside of Tibet, and at 8,000 feet above sea level, any vigorous activity left me gasping for breath in the early weeks, but it was a marvellous experience in so many ways. G taught all the sciences to the children of engineers who were building a dam high in the Peruvian mountains. I began teaching yoga to the wives of the engineers. I had developed my skills after a brief introductory yoga teachers' course in the UK. The classes in Peru didn't even need a village hall. The climate was so warm and the weather so fine that we could hold them on the extensive flat roof of our house. We were able to return to the UK having saved a goodly sum and quickly became the proud owners of a solid granite cottage in Cornwall. It boasted a garden, a stream and a field and had, in the words of the estate agent 'great potential'. It was a dream come true for Gerry and me. I'd had a second son in Peru and now, back home, our little family embraced the joys of country living.

To me it was back to my roots – I had been blessed with a rural childhood, having spent my first seven years on a farm on the edge of Exmoor. Those early years were idyllic. I think of the armfuls of bluebells we collected in the wood, the primroses and the lilacs in the orchard, and glimpses of foxes, badgers and deer in the fields. I met and played with the fairies that lived in a particular double tree-lined hedge that bordered our field and the moor, and I continued to keep them company at home, as they also lived on the wallpaper in my bedroom! I've never been quite sure if they were a figment of my imagination, but they were real enough to me at the time. I was never lonely on that isolated farm – I had my fairy friends, more about them in Part 2 of this book.

I was overjoyed to get back to rural life now that we had our own country cottage, which provided my husband with just the chance he needed to use his creative skills. He had the ability to visualise in detail how a building could be improved and the know-how to make his vision become a reality. Although he had no formal training in construction, he turned the cottage, with its tiny damp kitchen, three pokey living rooms and three bedrooms, into a comfortable four-bedroom home. He created a lovely south-facing, decent-sized sitting room and, with the help of a couple of builder friends from his choir, a beautiful big airy kitchen/dining room with an abundance of light. Two patios leading to the garden completed the transformation. Every change brought new joys for the family, and especially for me. G was not afraid of hard work. He was an excellent science teacher, much sought-after, but his ambition was to make a living as a landscape painter. Through selling his paintings he was able to leave his full-time post in a comprehensive school and take a part-time post as a physics teacher in a local private convent school. This gave him more time to focus on his painting. His landscape paintings had always earned him a reasonable amount of money, even in his days as a student. He decided to give up teaching three years after our return from Peru and make his living as an artist, painting in oils. I had every faith in him. Although we were bumping along the lower end of the earnings scale, we were still able to afford to make the changes to our home, all for the cost of bags of cement and other materials. The biggest ingredient was G's time and determination. We had a friend who was familiar with the grants that were available to home owners and, importantly for us, grants were being awarded for roof replacements. We managed to obtain one and were able to re-roof the house. Joy of joys… was that the angels working for us? That thought never once entered my mind until today as I reminisce, having had several possibly angelic interventions since that time.

I set up a playgroup in the local village, recruiting some other young mums to help me. This made me a number of friends and also gave my boys the company and friendship they needed. I fitted a child's seat to the back of my bike to take the younger boy with me wherever I went. Happy days!

G's oil painting skills developed quickly, his income from the pictures rapidly overtook his earnings as a teacher. He held exhibitions every two years in the Barbican Gallery in Plymouth, and many local people commissioned paintings from him. His images of cattle and sheep, misty rivers and sunsets, moorland and woodland scenes attracted popular acclaim. At the same time he interspersed the building work with trips to the pub to pick the brains of the local builders. He was popular because he had could talk to anyone and everyone, and his musical skills – playing the piano and piano accordion, and singing in and conducting the local male voice choir – made it easy for him to lead the singing in any pub. These are things the Cornish welcome and adore.

Moving on to our life after a dozen or so years in our cottage, both G and I began to take an interest in the numinous – a lovely word which covers everything that is 'scientifically' inexplicable and could be 'mystical' or related to 'God'.

The messages from the spiritualist medium G had received at the Christian Spiritualist Church, about the stack of papers in the wheelbarrow, were so accurate that it sparked his interest in the spiritual world. In our conversations about these matters with like-minded friends, all sorts of New Age books were recommended and lent to us. Books by authors such as Deepak Chopra, Osho, Neil Donald Walsh and James Redfield came our way. We began to devour these books on spirituality, searching for something convincing and tangible. We were sceptical but open. We both had degrees in science subjects and had trained to be biology teachers. It was hard to put aside normal logic, provable by scientific observation, and we did not ever do that, but we were willing to observe and take note of anything inexplicable by normal standards.

When we heard about a local Mind, Body and

Spirit festival, where fire-walking was on offer as an activity, G's eyes lit up. He thought that this was something that we could do together and that it might re-kindle the spark in our relationship, that in my case was sputtering somewhat. Not unusual for middle-aged women whose hormones start to dip, but G was definitely a fixer, and hoped to fix me.

To me the fire-walk would be some sort of proof that we were not just flesh and blood. There seemed to be something mystical about it and that was what I was after – more mystical proof. At the festival, we spent a couple of hours of preparation and meditation with the fire-walk teacher. Then we all walked across to a big bonfire of sizeable logs which were glowing red, the flames having died down. We watched the Shaman and some helpers rake the hot cinders to form a deep, burning carpet of 'coals' five metres long and two metres wide. Then one after another, twenty of us walked barefoot along it. It was a very uplifting and empowering experience. The actual feeling in our feet was of walking on a crunchy carpet, we felt no heat at all. We were unscathed. We repeated the event the following year with our two boys who were by this time sixteen and eighteen. The youngest, always very laid-back, strolled slowly over the coals and was as completely unburnt as we were, after our fairly fast-paced walk!

Even more fascinating for G was witnessing the fire-walk Shaman, John Shango, walk across a carpet strewn with a sackful of roughly broken bottles. This was the Glass Walk. He did not allow his acolytes to participate. To risk being burnt was one thing, but to achieve the kind of mind-over-matter power to walk over shards of broken bottles was a step further on. What did it all mean? We never really knew. To me it seemed to indicate that we are more than mere flesh and blood. I found that very exciting and affirming. It did seem to buck us up spiritually speaking, but it did not bring about the changes in me that G had hoped for..

For many years I saw the fire-walk as a proof of humans being more than mere physical bodies, but some clever scientists have proposed a theory about why people can walk on red-hot coals unharmed. The theory involves evaporation of sweat. I don't really believe it, but I have to acknowledge that it could be true. I do wonder, however, how many of them would dare to walk over red-hot coals to prove that theirs was the correct explanation of the phenomenon. Neither can I get out of my mind seeing pictures of 'extreme' Indian yogis hanging from hooks in their flesh with no apparent pain or ill effect on their bodies. That can't be explained by glib assertions that they have hypnotised themselves, or can it?

I have been asked why I was looking for 'mystical proof'. To those who are not 'seekers' I will explain. Mankind has always reached beyond this physical world to understand the whys and wherefores of our fascinating and sometimes very difficult lives.

In other words, I can't help asking questions and looking for answers that I can believe in, and I continue to do so.

~ CHAPTER 5 ~

Zambia

A shocking event that made me wonder about 'angelic rescues'

I need to go back in time to explain the dreadful situation that first made me think we might be being looked after by forces other than normal human ones, like the police and the fire brigade.

At the age of twenty-one, I was studying for a Post Graduate Certificate in Education (PGCE) to teach biology in secondary schools. This course was split in two, divided by a year when I went abroad on Voluntary Service Overseas (VSO). In the first term at Nottingham University, I spent my time attending lectures and in teaching practice. I was sent to an unruly comprehensive school and given the hardest classes to teach. The classroom noise was appalling and the kids had no intention whatsoever of listening to me. I had decided to teach seed dispersal, a subject I found fascinating, all the more so because it involved looking at plant materials and drawing things. *What a treat!* I thought... All I remember about the lessons was the pitch of my own voice – unusually high. Even the experience of that unruly class didn't put me off wanting to be a teacher, as I knew that soon I would be abroad in a warm country far away from the grime and drizzle of Nottingham.

In January 1972 I went to Zambia as a VSO to spend a year teaching at a Methodist ministry girls' school in Choma – a very small provincial town in the middle of the bush in Southern Zambia. I was employed to teach agriculture and biology to girls in a school of about 200 pupils. The girls were model students. They couldn't have been better behaved. They truly valued education and that made my job much easier. I learned a great deal about myself and the world in that year. G and I had spent every weekend together for the whole of the previous year at his student rental in an outlying village of Nottingham. We had considered getting married, but I decided to continue with my plan to go on VSO because we both thought that at twenty-one and twenty-three we were too young to settle down. We parted. He wrote to me regularly however and I replied. He became very lonely and was missing me. My letters to him indicated that I was having a great time, which I was, in the sense that I was experiencing new things, like horse riding in the bush and so on, but there was still a place in my heart for him.

In April 1972, Gerry proposed to me by letter from England. I couldn't just say yes, but I agreed that he should come out to see me, which is what he planned to do. He painted thirty oil paintings, a major achievement, in the time between writing to me in April and coming out to see me in August, during the Zambian schools' holidays. He sold all the canvases and managed to scrape together enough money to get as far as Nairobi airport, in Kenya. It was reckoned to be five days away by bus from Lusaka, the capital of Zambia. There was no transport to take him on to Choma and he had no money left, so he set out to walk and hitch lifts.

It was a dangerous journey and Gerry had no more than a tennis racket to protect himself. He survived a couple of very scary incidents on the way. Just outside Lusaka, at night, G was aware that he was being followed and there was nothing he could do about it. He was very fortunate in that a car driver, a South African man, realising the danger he was in, stopped to give him a lift. After a five-hour drive he arrived in Choma. It was good to see him. Within a few days he picked up his paints and used them to pay his way. He painted an elephant standing beside an anthill, a lovely picture. It was stolen by the man who had been good enough to give him the lift. The man, however, was not good enough to pay him for the picture that he took away 'on approval'! Perhaps in the man's mind G owed him something (possibly even his life) for picking him up in the dark along a lonely road, with a group of men following him. Perhaps he was right...

We settled in to a domestic pattern, I did the shopping and the cooking. G painted pictures and played squash with the local farmers. All was going well but, within three weeks of G's arrival, I was attacked and assaulted. I was alone, driving a little moped along a quiet road. I had been shopping in the market a couple of miles away from the school. It was a much corrugated and deeply sandy road through the bush, and the moped was laden with bags of fruit and vegetables. A man stepped out from the bush. He was waving his arms at me. It was in the middle of nowhere, low scrubby bushes fringed the roadside, and continued for miles across the wild countryside. The school was perhaps a mile away. I was driving very slowly in the deep sand, wondering what the man wanted.

"You have dropped something, madam," he shouted. He came forward, blocking my path. As I stopped the bike he grabbed it, and hit me on the head with a rock. It was a warning blow.

I won't go into details of the next five hours, what I will say is that they have stayed with me for the whole of my life, leaving me with fears no woman should have to suffer. The man told me of his hatred of white women and that his plan was to rob and assault me. He said he was a Zimbabwean terrorist. I thought that my saving grace would be to tell him the truth about myself, to appeal to his better nature. I told him I was not a rich white woman, but a volunteer teacher earning just enough to feed myself. I said I had come out to Zambia to help the local people; I was giving my service to them and he was rewarding me like this! I told him I did not deserve such treatment. I talked and talked, thinking that if he could begin to see me as a fellow human being instead of a hated white woman, he might release me.

After five long hours of being tied up and thinking about my possible fate, two local men wandered into the bush. My attacker spoke to them and ran away. I asked them what they were going to do with me, because the attacker had said he and his friends were going to decide whether or not to kill me. They denied knowing him, and I found I had to explain what had occurred. They appeared to be shocked, and did not hesitate to take me back to the school in their Land Rover.

Something happened to me that day. I think my mind shut down on the event. It was so terrifying that I became rather zombie-like. I managed to do everyday things, but looking back I believe I neglected some of my duties with my students. I hope none of them suffered too much as a result. I could have gone home, back to the UK, but I didn't want my parents to know about my ordeal – they might have blamed themselves for letting me go. I only had another three months left to serve. My confidence had been severely shaken, though, and I couldn't bear the thought of being alone in my house on the school grounds. The school could not condone G living 'in sin' with me, so we decided to get married. It was what he had wanted anyway, and I loved and admired him in so many ways, it felt like exactly the right thing to do.

At seven-thirty on a Wednesday morning in September, just before I taught a lesson in agriculture, we had an official marriage at the Boma (the Town Hall) in Choma. At the end of the school day the other VSOs organised a surprise wedding party in their house. Tears of gratitude filled my eyes. They had normalised the very difficult and unusual situation. They even made us a wedding cake! We married for a second time very soon after our return to the UK. My mother was not deprived of the joy of arranging a wedding for her only daughter and my parents never did find out about the Zambian wedding.

Sometimes I allowed myself to think about those two men who had rescued me. I recalled that they had said they were surveyors looking at the land. I often wondered if they were really angels, although I didn't believe in angels. It was such a coincidence that they had appeared in my hour of need and had rescued me and taken me home.

Of course, they could have been the attacker's accomplices, but how did they know exactly where I would be on that stretch of road? They seemed as surprised to see me as I was to see them. I will never know, but I'm eternally grateful to them, whoever they were. I do remember praying for help just in case anyone was listening. Perhaps they really were angels, sent to help me.

~ CHAPTER 6 ~

The Ouija Board

*A dangerous adventure which opened
a door that should have stayed shut*

At fourteen I was ready to explore the world, bold in my ignorance. I was even allowed to have boyfriends and to wear make-up. I made the mistake of the typical teenager – thinking I knew it all.

My three school friends and I heard about Ouija boards and were fascinated. These might at last indicate whether there was any truth in all the mumbo-jumbo type mysticism that one heard about. We honestly wanted to know the truth. I had been brought up a Catholic, although my mother was an atheist and my father was a very lapsed Catholic. They thought the church upbringing would be good for us, and in many ways it was. My brothers and I were sent to church for mass on Sundays for many years. We learned the Ten Commandments and knew right from wrong. The Ouija board never got a mention, though, so we thought it might be a good idea to try and test it out.

My friend laid out the letters of the alphabet in a circle around a central upturned wine glass on a smooth table. The four of us sat round with our fingers on the glass. We asked, "Is anyone there?" After several times of asking and false moves and giggles, the glass started to move. We were all serious girls, no one wished to cheat or pretend to the others that things were happening when they were not. The glass moved with surprising speed and accuracy. There would have been no time to co-ordinate our fingers and plan out letters. Some strange names started to form and some peculiar messages came, for no one in particular. Then a named entity spelt out "Bugger off!" Shrieks of laughter from us all and a certain amount of shock spurred us on to start asking questions.

Someone asked if there were any messages for any of us. The glass indicated "YES."

We asked "Who for?"

The answer was "TESSA."

We asked, "Who are you?"

The answer was "BARBARA."

I asked "Where are you?"

The answer was "STOCKPORT."

By this time I was feeling very uncomfortable indeed, no one else knew my friend Barbara who had moved to Stockport.

Someone asked "What do you want to say to Tessa?"

The glass spelt out…"Y.O.U. W.E.R.E. C.R.U…" I took my hand off the glass. I was horrified. I knew what the other letters would be. I was CRUEL! I had never intended to be cruel, but it was true I had been. Barbara had been a close and lovely friend during my last year at primary school. In the holidays she'd shown me a book her parents had given her. It was a young person's guide to sex education. I was shocked, but at the same time I couldn't help being fascinated. The Church would not have approved, I thought. My parents never spoke about such things; it seemed to me that it was all a shameful secret. Barbara wanted to act out the boyfriend and girlfriend scenes. We used to spend our playground time riding imaginary horses, but this was a different kind of imaginary activity and I wanted none of it. She kissed my hand and touched me. At that point I really freaked out.

I didn't visit her house again. The summer holidays ended and I went off to the local grammar school. There was Barbara, walking up the road, past my house to the new school. My blood ran cold and I turned away from her. Fortunately she was not in my class, but I couldn't bring myself to talk to her or even look at her. I cut her out of my life. It was as if she represented a great sin. I was cruel in that sense. Poor Barbara. Her family moved away to Stockport at some time in that first year of secondary school. Now here she was, rebuking me via the Ouija board, two years after we had started at the grammar school. Was she speaking from the grave or via a spirit by proxy? I have never discovered the truth of that matter.

That day I cycled home faster than ever before, fearing I was possibly being chased by demons. I told my mother and slept with her in her bed for the first time since I'd been a young child. My mother didn't believe in ghosts, and comforted me, though she couldn't explain what had taken place. She just advised me not to use a Ouija board again, and I wholeheartedly agreed! I never heard anything about Barbara again. As an adult I tried searching for her online in Friends Reunited, and later on Facebook, but there was no sign of her anywhere. I wanted to apologise to her.

That was really my first actual proof of other realms, unless I include the fairies on our farm. But I could never be sure about those slippery little creatures!

I have since learned that the kinds of spirit that can come through a Ouija board may be of a very low order, with bad motivations and ill intent. They may be stuck on the 'Earth plane' and be looking for ways to express themselves through human energy. Horror stories may reflect their activities, or may be extreme exaggerations of what they can do. It is considered very unwise to offer these spirits any opportunity to come into our lives. I do not think my childhood friend was in any way demonic, and the fact that she came through to me seems to indicate that there are other, less sinister energies using the board to communicate. The risk is too great, however, I would strongly advise against experimenting with a Ouija board. It's playing with fire...

~ CHAPTER 7 ~

Meditation Circles

The path to enlightenment started here in a strange and captivating way

At around the time I was attending the healing course in Plymouth, G and I were invited to join a spiritual development meditation circle, in which one seeks spiritual guidance from a teacher, and from spirit guides that may come along. It was run by a wonderful woman, Lynda Norris, a member of my yoga class. She was three years my junior and said she had always been psychic. She had practised as a medium, and had taught a lot of people about the spiritual side of life. I liked what she said; I thought her ideas about reincarnation and philosophy were very sound. I could never accept the Christian idea that we have only one go at life and when we're dead, that's it. Life gone. End of story. Off we go to heaven or hell, for ever; or possibly to purgatory, a place of suffering but eventual redemption, according to the Catholic Church. What about all the unfortunate people who die at a very early age through no fault of their own? I could go on.

Lynda, the medium, told us that we have many lives. Each life has a purpose or several purposes. We are here to learn all sorts of aspects of living. When we come into this world we come knowingly, having been helped to make a decision by our guides and angels as to the best next life for us. Lynda was not dogmatic. Different people have different truths. A Hindu, Muslim, Jew or Christian will have their own interpretations of the end-of-life story. No one can really say that one is right and another is wrong, it's just that, to me, some ideas seem to make more sense than others.

G and I attended this circle once a fortnight for four years. It was a great joy and a wonderful experience and twice brought to me people in spirit who have changed my life in very positive ways. On one of these occasions, I mentally sent up a question to the Universe. I had so many New-Age books to read, and very few of them made any sense to me, so I asked, *What should I read?* Seraphina (my guardian angel) appeared in meditation as a collection of points of light, and I recognised her 'energy'. I had met her before this appearance. I need to say that so many mystical happenings were occurring at this time that it is hard to avoid taking the reader by surprise, so when I talk about Seraphina, be patient, I will explain later.

"Come with me," she said, taking me by the hand and up into the dark sky, across continents, until we reached a snow-capped mountain range.

"These are the Himalayas", she told me. We went down to a craggy rock face, where we found an opening, the entrance to a cave. Inside sat a guru, cross-legged and wearing a mustard-yellow robe.

Answering my question, he recommended, "Read the Upanishads and the Bhagavad Gita. There you will find what you need to know." He was talking about texts that I had read during my three-year yoga teachers' diploma qualification. They had meant little to me at the time. We left the guru and returned to the room. It's amazing how fast you can travel in meditation! I dutifully re-read those books over the next few weeks, but their significance was still no clearer to me than it had been fifteen years before.

Three weeks later I was preparing a class for my yoga students, trying to think of something to tell them about the chakras. I had no idea at all what to say. I decided to meditate and ask for help. Although I had not anticipated him, the same guru from the Himalayas appeared in my mind.

"You should not be teaching your people spiritual practices unless they are following the *Yamas* and *Niyamas*," he said.

Again, this was something that I had learnt about in my yoga teachers' course, the *Yamas* and *Niyamas* are the 'rules of life', the moral code. They are similar to the Ten Commandments in the Bible. Embarrassed, I could only think of two out of ten of the rules – non-violence and truthfulness.

The guru's voice was stern, "You are a yoga teacher, you should know the laws of life!" He then became gentle and kind, and said reassuringly: "Never mind. I will help you," and he gave me a story about himself as a small child, wanting more than his fair share of the special sweets! I had a pen in my hand, paper at the ready, and I was able to 'hear' his dictation and write down every word.

I was astonished. It was an appealing little story – perfectly formed. I hadn't written stories since I was twelve years old, and then only when required to write essays for school. I had no thoughts or ambitions to be a story writer and wondered what I should do with the story. Then I realised it would be ideal to read out to the yoga class. It was amusing, gentle and appropriate, because it was about greed – what the Bible calls gluttony. In our affluent society, greed is a failing of many of us, including myself and many of my class members. Most of us were slightly, or in some cases considerably, overweight. The guru had just given me a way of tackling teaching the laws (or rules) of life to people who were much older than I was, and in many cases wiser too! Over days, weeks and months I continued to receive stories from the guru that began to cover other subjects in yoga, but not before my meeting with a Native American Chief.

In our meditation circle sometimes we picked up messages for each other. One evening, after our meditation, one of the young men in the group sat up and looked at me and in a rather puzzled way.

"Tessa, I have a horse for you," he said. "Perhaps that means something to you?"

All I could say was "Thank you, I've no idea about that. I'm not a horsey person." There was some debate about whether it was a symbol of power or energy now offered to me, those being attributes of the horse (in traditional Indigenous beliefs, different animals represent different traits, eg a deer represents gentleness and so on).

At the next meditation evening, I saw a Native American chief with a full head-dress of feathers. People often talk about 'Indian chiefs' in spiritual circles and here I was seeing one for myself. As usual I was sceptical and thought I had dreamt him up, but in my vision he seemed so big, important and detailed, that I felt I needed to find out more.

"You can always meditate a second time to follow up visions and discover more about them," Lynda suggested. I had been learning how to do channelled drawing. This is achieved by holding a pen on a piece of paper and letting the pen do the drawing. The right procedures have to be followed. The next evening, after he appeared to me in the circle, I asked if the chief would show himself to me in some way. My husband was sitting at the table at the time. I went into meditation and I found myself drawing clear, slow lines which initially looked like fingers. As more lines appeared, a picture emerged of an upside-down face.

I turned the picture the right way up, and saw that I had drawn the profile of a Native American chief with a large feathered head-dress. I allowed my pen to continue moving and the words 'Calling Horse' were spelled out. I took this to be the picture and the name of my Indian chief. This came as a huge surprise to both me and Gerry, I had never produced a channelled drawing before. The fact that it was upside down added to the intrigue. Normal life continued unchanged, except for a little more openness to other realms perhaps.

Calling Horse channelled drawing

The chief had come to be available to me. I pondered over how he might be able to help me. I had read a book, *The Gospel of the Red Man* by Earnest Thomas Seaton, who had mentioned twelve Native American Laws of Life. I wanted to compare them to the laws from my Indian guru. I decided to ask the chief about the laws of his people. Over time, Calling Horse gave me a beautiful set of stories about a way of life I knew nothing of. When I published them online, a Native American man responded immediately and said he loved the stories. That was a relief to me, as they are quite detailed regarding customs and I didn't know these traditions at all.

I could believe these things because they actually happened to me. When Lynda told us about her spiritual happenings, which she did occasionally, I could not take them on board. They seemed beyond belief to me. Not that I thought she was disingenuous, it was just not my truth. I think blind faith can be a dangerous thing; it can lead to people being duped and swindled and made to feel foolish. You have to find your own truth, but you also have to WANT to find it. It is this 'wanting' that makes a difference.

'Spirit' seems to respond to those who have the DESIRE to know.

Lynda was very insistent that we should always reach for the highest possible source of information when we are asking for help.

There is a procedure that we learnt to follow that goes like this:

1. Sit quietly and relax. Visualise a symbol of your deity – it could be Jesus, Buddha, or any other god, or Universal energy, or the Source, perhaps a Yin Yang symbol, or the OM (the Yoga symbol for the Godhead), or your own Higher Self, which is part of the greater divinity.

2. Ask to be surrounded in love and light, and picture it as a shining barrier to any negativity.

3. Imagine yourself growing roots of energy into the ground, deep into the earth (known as 'grounding yourself' which has the effect of holding the energetic body of the meditator in a stable, Earthbound state).

4. Then you are ready to meditate and receive.

5. To close down after meditation, you can visualise each chakra shrinking to a small point of light, and once again become aware of the contact of your feet with the floor.

Lynda taught us that we are in control; nothing can get through to us that we don't want. Lower levels of existence are more able to get through to us when we use physical means, such as pen pushed channelling (in the way I described when the Calling Horse picture came to me) and dowsing. We were warned to beware of these methods, but I found it all absolutely fascinating. Through the pen I also made contact with a guide called Niasco. He seemed to be some kind of Roman soldier. His advice was sound. After three sessions I asked him if it would be possible to increase my psychic energy. He told me it would be possible, and that I could contact a different entity, which he named, for that information. He warned me, though, that this spirit was 'not always a good spirit'. I decided, of course, that I would not be contacting this entity.

On my next session, I opened up and protected myself as Lynda had taught us, put my pen to paper and the marking started. It felt different. It was tight and small compared to Niasco's writing, which was large and loose. I asked for a name and nothing happened. I asked a second and a third time. I had been told that on the third asking the spirit would be required to give their name. The name that came was that of the entity the Roman soldier had mentioned, who was 'not always a good spirit'. To this day I will not mention the name of that spirit. I threw my pen across the room and surrounded myself in love and light as much as possible. Quite shaken, I phoned my teacher. She reiterated the dangers of such a physical method of contact with Spirit and I decided that I would not use that method any more; I would stick to meditation. Meditation comes through at a much higher level and can be controlled by refusing to entertain any negative thoughts or ideas, by simply stopping, grounding oneself and doing something different.

I have attended three meditation groups, and

finally I ran one of my own. They were all quite different in their aims. Lynda's group was about personal spiritual development – dead relatives did not appear. The objective of the second group, that I attended only once, seemed to be just about opening up in meditation and seeing what happened, in order to prove to people that we could be in contact with 'the other side'. I decided to meditate in turn for each person in the group, so that I could pick up something that would be helpful to each one. The strategy was successful in that the messages I received were accurate. One such message was from a mother in the spirit world to her daughter, who was meditating with us in the room. I reported what I had seen to her:

"I saw a ribbon bow with wedding bells, but it didn't seem to be about a wedding. Does that mean anything to you?" The woman beamed, then dabbed her eyes.

"For about twenty years I have been wearing a gold bow and bells round my neck. My mother gave it to me as a wedding present. I took it off last week because it was making a mark on my skin when I lay in the sun. I wanted an even tan! Mother passed away last year."

Turning to a younger woman I said, "I saw a young girl sitting down having her dark-coloured fringe snipped at by a pair of very busy scissors, held by an impatient hand."

Her face lit up, "My grandma was a hairdresser. She was always complaining about how fast my fringe grew, and she would quickly snip it off before I had time to escape."

The last one that I remember was for a worried-looking man. I saw a small set of purple curtains, the sort you see opening in a crematorium to let a body through to the fire chamber. That posed a dilemma for me. I didn't know whether I should tell him or not, and I had no clue as to whether it was a prediction about him or someone close to him, or something else entirely. I made as light as I could of it, but I felt concerned about giving such a message. The man seemed to receive it calmly enough, but did not know what it was about. I was not a trained medium and neither did I want to be. I left the group thinking that it was not for me as I already knew that there is a spirit realm, and I felt no particular need to make contact with it.

In the third meditation group that I belonged to for a few years, we were given a variety of spiritual journeys by the teacher and introduced to a number of gods and goddesses, I enjoyed the meditations, and indeed one of the deities did make an appearance in my life several years later. In my own group I wanted to show the participants different forms of meditation, of which, more later…

Summing up, through the meditation circles, some more tangible proofs of other levels of existence had appeared. By this time I was of course not a sceptic at all, but I will continue to list my proofs for the benefit of those who do not believe, to show them happenings which actually convinced other people, for example, members of my meditation group and my husband. I hope that this will encourage readers to be open, to do their own safe investigating and find their own answers.

~ CHAPTER 8 ~

Healing Body, Mind and Spirit – Mine and Others

Some dramatic happenings
during healing sessions

As part of my healing course at Unity house in Plymouth, I was encouraged to practise giving healing energy to people I knew – friends and family. This practice enabled me to become familiar with the array of states that the chakras could exhibit, and as a healer, to feel those different energies in my hands. We could also get feedback from our 'patients', by asking how it felt for them, and what happened, if anything, during the healing. I worked with a number of people, most of whom were normal healthy, happy individuals. Healing works on all levels – physical, mental, emotional and spiritual. Some of my 'patients' had had big issues in their lives; these were the ones who taught me the most.

A man with a heart condition offered himself as a guinea pig. He was a pleasant but extremely talkative man, who interrupted his wife at every turn. He could feel a large amount of heat coming from my hands, although to touch they seemed cool. When I felt his chakras his throat centre was huge, his heart centre tiny, if not closed. His sacral (sexual) energy centre was closed. I gave him healing on several occasions, but didn't burden him with my knowledge about the state of his chakras. I felt that although I could learn from this healing experience, his behaviour was so entrenched, and his illness so established, that I could do little to help him except to offer emotional support, which he did appreciate. As his wife was very spiritually inclined and had a psychic daughter, I decided to discuss her husband with her, in order to learn more about the workings of the chakras in real life. His life history was sad, but for me, his history and the state of his chakras was very informative.

His childhood was beset with three deaths in the family. His mother, father and brother all died before he was fifteen. This would explain the state of his heart chakra. He was afraid of the loss of love, so he was afraid to love. His mother had died in childbirth when he was fourteen. In his subconscious mind he associated sex (i.e. reproduction) with death. He and his now wife had waited to start their sexual life until after their marriage (the second time for both of them). He was impotent, and had known that he was. His wife was bitter about that. She felt he had duped her. He was the sort of man who was quite flirtatious and implied sexual interest in his conversations. His throat chakra seemed to be compensating for the lack of energy in his sexual centre. A crude analysis could express this as 'all mouth and no trousers'!

This phenomenon was described in Brennan's book, where one chakra expands, compensating for a lack of energy in another. It can happen in a number of different ways. For example, when a powerful person, who has a very large solar plexus energy (denoting personal power), is incapable of loving for whatever reason, their heart chakra is likely to be small, closed, or even negative. Power and ambition can over-ride compassion. These people could be described as 'heart-less'.

See Appendix 1 for a simple explanation of the significance of the main chakras.

Another client, Nick. came to me, a man who, after his third attempt at suicide, had been told that there was a waiting list for counselling of at least six weeks. I had not yet started my counselling and psychotherapy diploma, that was to come later, so I really did not know whether I would be any use to this poor fellow. I agreed to try to help him as he was the brother of a close friend of mine and the family really seemed desperate.

I had learnt that one could analyse people's chakras remotely, by meditating and using a pendulum – tuning in to them. In Nick's absence, I tuned in to his chakras and discovered that they were very negative, with some being more closed than others. I then had a meeting with him and found him to be a pleasant, if anxious, man, keen to look for solutions. I thought I could cope with his energy and his presence. At first I just gave him healing. Nearly all his chakras responded well and he started feeling much better. But there seemed to be two chakras that were blocked. I was beginning to think that it was necessary to become pro-active with the healing, in other words to direct my attention to specific chakras. This was not a good plan and had some dramatic consequences, as you will see. I have since learnt that it is better to let the healing occur at a pace guided by the healing energy itself, or the Universe, rather than trying to 'push' it to correct specific areas. "Just let it flow," was the mantra, "it will go to where it is most needed."

I had followed all the usual protections and commenced the healing. On previous occasions with this man, he had been sitting in a chair and I had stood beside him and moved round his aura, passing the healing energy through my hands and into his energy system. Sometimes people lie on a couch for healing. Nick sat in the same way, on a chair on this occasion, but in a different room and fortunately, as it turned out, with a lot of space around him. The warm sunshine was streaming through the French window, and everything seemed fine and relaxed, when suddenly he was overtaken with a terrible pain in his abdomen and his chest. He needed to lie down.

I put a blanket on the floor and he curled up into the fetal position, seemingly in agony. I asked if I should phone the ambulance and he came out of his trance and said no, he would be okay, then he went back to the agony. I asked the same question again twice more, but he was determined that it would pass. He was going through something that only he could see. I was kneeling beside him with my hands in his aura praying for the energy to help him, and praying that God would not let him die, which in my inexperience did look like a possibility. The session went on for forty-five minutes. Suddenly he relaxed, smiled and told me about the most astonishing events that he witnessed during his very painful reverie. It seemed that the healing had dislodged memories from his energy field, things that had apparently happened to him in past lives. The first was a flaying, a punishment, brutally administered. The second was a death, a sword plunged into his solar plexus. That he had apparently been witnessing his past lives, would, to me, be an indicator that reincarnation is 'a thing'.

This man was a Catholic, had attended a Catholic school and had been beaten on many occasions by the monks, in his childhood. He hated them and resented their treatment of him and the other boys.

His relationship of ten years with a woman whom he loved had failed, much to his deep regret. In life he overcame his issues by projecting himself as a very jokey person whom nobody would suspect was feeling suicidal. In an effort to help him relax, he had become a chain-smoker.

Gradually, over time and with some more healing sessions, he became 'light' and well again, but a problem occurred. This was something I had not heard about until I did my counselling diploma. It's called transference. There are several forms of it, but the transference that I experienced on this occasion was that of my client falling in love with me. He was feeling absolutely terrible about it. He knew it was completely inappropriate both for him and for me, and he decided that we should have no more healing sessions. I was distraught, because he seemed to have been getting on so well, he seemed to be on the verge of a great new life but he was wavering, and I felt responsible for him. We were both in what may be described as 'a right old state'!

I decided to tell my husband about this therapeutic disaster. In floods of tears I confessed what had happened.

"That's bad," he said. "You didn't see that one coming, did you? Poor Nick, I hope you haven't actually made him worse off than before. I don't know what to suggest. Why don't you sleep on it and it might look better by the morning?"

That same night, at midnight, I was lying in bed unable to sleep. Tears were flowing down my cheeks, I was so upset and worried for Nick. As I lay on my bed I saw above me the misty face of a beautiful woman, with large dark eyes and long black hair parted in the middle. She wore a royal-blue gown. She placed her hands on the sides of my face, and then on my brow. They felt so comforting. She said clearly to me in a voice I heard internally:

"Don't worry, we will take this problem away

from you." The vision of her faded away, and her touch seemed to linger on my face. Suddenly I felt totally uplifted, a huge weight was gone from my chest. I felt elated. I ran downstairs to tell Gerry, who was doing some late-night painting. He didn't know what to make of my experience, but he looked relieved, and very glad to see that I was too.

The next day Nick appeared at our house, looking anxious. I told him about my visitation; my angel. He was delighted for me and for us both. He seemed to have had some sort of spiritual revelation as well. He continued his healing path elsewhere and eventually returned to the arms of his beloved Christian Church, which gave him the comfort he needed. Nick became a force for good in the area where he lived, helping other people in need. His was a happy ending after many years of suffering.

I had met an angel. Another proof to me that help exists on planes invisible to us, but which are there nevertheless and able to manifest, should the need arise. I have since read that angels like and want to be asked for help. If we shut them out, they may not appear in our time of trouble. If there is a life-or-death situation, they have been reported to swoop in and avert disaster sometimes. However, I cannot vouch for that, as it is only something I have read about and I am always looking for actual felt or seen proof!

The past-life experience with Nick was very intriguing, and although I did not ever encounter another case of it during healing sessions, I did go to two different practitioners myself. One was a past-life healer and the other a hypnotherapist. My hope was to solve one of my own issues – the one related to my Zambian experience. Strangely, both sessions brought to the fore traumatic issues related to the sacral chakra in previous lives, one of which had occurred many hundreds of years ago. It was a complex tale of my historical, brutal husband and of me seeking the help of a 'wise woman'. In that life I already had five young children, and I knew that she could help me to prevent any more pregnancies. This prevention involved a tool that held a hot cinder being inserted into me then removed quickly. I saw a clear picture of this device which was like a set of tongs, but with three arms that worked together to hold the cinder. I was told to refuse my husband's sexual attentions until the wound healed. I had to confess to him that I had visited the wise woman and had the treatment. As a result, my husband not only raped me but he'd also reported me to the priest. I was forced to have a pillory punishment, and my own death came soon after, from an infection passed on to me by my husband in that ancient life.

This all came to me while I was in a deep hypnotic trance, but still able to hear the therapist's questions and to answer them as the story unfolded to me. I don't consider it to be proof of anything, but it was certainly interesting, and food for thought. I have not had the misfortune to experience brutality in any of my marriages in this life, for which I am very grateful.

During my counselling course, many techniques from all sorts of different modes of talking therapies were employed. One of these appeared to have a deep spiritual effect on me. My teachers were interested in Shamanism, and one day they offered us a deep meditation session accompanied by the regular beat of a drum. The session was a guided 'inner journey', meaning that while one of the teachers drummed, the other talked us through a journey of the mind, involving rivers, bridges and crystal-lined caves. While in the cave I saw a royal-blue, eye-shaped light glowing in the centre of my forehead. It was persistent throughout the rest of the meditation and only disappeared when we 'came back into the room'. When I shared this experience with the group, my teacher said that perhaps I had opened my third eye. I was pleased, as this is mentioned a lot in spiritual writings, and seems to be important for one's spiritual growth. After that I often saw my third eye when I was meditating. Over the years, it has changed from a royal-blue to a lime/emerald-green eye shape, surrounded by royal blue, with the colours swirling and changing place over and over again. It seems to have settled to a solid green these days and it is round rather than eye-shaped.

~ CHAPTER 9 ~

More About the Healing Course at Unity House, Plymouth

Healing becomes a reality

The healing course was a great revelation to me. There were about ten students, ranging in age from mid-forties (I was forty-five) to seventies. In recent years the course has become academic as well as spiritual. Now, only those capable of quite a lot of studying will be able to gain accreditation. It was not like that when I was a student on the course.

All course members worked with each other throughout; we made sure that we experienced the healing touch of everyone else. I will never forget a charming elderly gentleman, a retired manual worker with little or no education, giving me healing during the course. Receiving this man's energy felt like being in an electric field so powerful that I could feel it all over my body. It was rather similar to the pull of a magnet, or perhaps the opposite of that – when the two north poles of magnets are put together. He was a man of few words and very gentle in character. It would be a great shame if people, gifted in the way that he was, could not use their gift. However, he may not have been looking to become a 'professional' healer, but simply to give healing to those in need who came to his attention, and that is really what healing is about.

At the start of the healing sessions, we learnt how to protect ourselves and our patients by 'seeing' them and ourselves surrounded in Love and Light from the Highest Source, or God. We were shown how to tune in to the Universal Source of energy and channel it to the other person. We learned not to give our own energy to anybody else, because that could result in us becoming ill or burnt-out. We learnt the significance of the chakras and the aura to the biology of the human body. We learnt about warning signs of ill health and when to advise the client to see a doctor. It was very important not to make the client feel dependent on the healer. We were advised to undertake a counselling course, to avoid the temptation of giving the client the 'benefit of our experience' ie. telling the client about what happened to us in what we perceive to be similar circumstances This is entirely the wrong thing to do, because experience can vary so widely. I realised that I had made that very mistake myself. We were encouraged to practise with as many people as possible. It could be difficult to interpret the strength or pressure of a chakra as, in some cases, a big pressure could mean the chakra was strongly positive, and in others it could mean it was strongly negative. I discovered that ambiguity in one of my patients whom I knew to be averse to intimacy, but whose sacral chakra felt very strong to the touch. I realised it meant the chakra was strongly negative. I also came across a man who could hardly utter a word, but whose throat energy felt very powerful – powerfully negative was my final conclusion, after realising that he could not express himself verbally.

We learnt how to ground ourselves. Grounding is a strange concept perhaps to those with no experience of spiritual matters. One can become quite detached from the world, and even literally dizzy or unbalanced, if one does not close down properly after spiritual activities. I certainly learnt that from experience! On one occasion I was talking to a young woman who was fascinated by the subject of healing. We were in a cafe for a long time, drinking cups of herb tea and eating cake slowly. When I stood up to visit the bathroom I felt as if I had slipped sideways out of my aura. I had to hold on to the wall to keep my balance. I went through a grounding procedure to correct things, but it was a bit disconcerting at the time! I did not tell the young woman about this experience as I didn't want to put her off her interest in this important subject. I was grateful I had been warned on the course about the effect of not closing down properly and had been given the tools to deal with it should it occur. I never had a repeat of that bad experience.

Closing down involves a combination of surrounding oneself in an aura of white light, deliberately imagining each chakra closing to a mere point of light, and grounding oneself by creating an imagined energy link to the earth – the roots growing down as described before.

We were taught to cleanse our energies by washing our hands after giving healing, and picture cutting the energetic ties between ourselves and the client. It's no good carrying clients in one's head all day long and fretting about them. That would be very draining for the healer and would not help the client at all. Opening up and closing down are essential parts of the healer's skills.

On the Plymouth course, the teacher gave us the opportunity to meet our guardian angel or spirit guide. Some people recognised the guide who came to them. I was going to have to wait to meet my angel, and she did indeed come to me when I needed saving from the situation with Nick, my client. When I saw my angel the second time, though she did not show herself to me as a 'person', I recognised her sparkling energy and I asked her what she was called. She told me her name was Seraphina. I had never ever given any thought to this name. It had never been on the tip of my tongue or anywhere in my mind, but it sounded exactly right and I loved it, and still do.

The teacher on our course thought we would benefit from learning about dowsing and using a pendulum (usually a crystal on a fine chain) to measure chakras on the body of the patient. This could be done over a patient lying on a massage couch, fully clothed and relaxing. The pendulum describes circles of differing sizes, for example, in a wide-open chakra, a saucer-sized circle may be shown, and in a more closed chakra the circle may be the size of a hazelnut. Other patterns indicating other activities of the chakras do show themselves and are well illustrated in Barbara Ann Brennan's book, *The Hands of Light*. A pendulum can also be useful when there is no other easy way to discover something. However, a pendulum can be tricky to use. I found that I should only ask it about things that don't matter to me personally, for example, choosing essential oils or crystals for a particular purpose. They don't matter in the sense that I have no fixed opinion about them, and a wrong choice does not lead to disaster. Questions such as 'Should I marry this man?' or 'Is this person trustworthy?' or 'Should I buy this house, or take this new job?' are all inappropriate questions for a pendulum!

See Appendix 2 for more information on my use of the pendulum

After my two-year course on 'spiritual or natural healing' and a great deal of practising on clients, with varying degrees of 'success', I was asked if I would like to teach the course myself. Our facilitator was leaving, and the Healing Centre needed another person to present the course to replace him. I was already a trained teacher, familiar with presenting lessons and classes to adults, and I had had much more practice with clients than the average newly trained healer, because I wasn't having to go to work to earn a crust every day. I had also developed several unexpected spiritual abilities that are described in this book. So, after some debate with my husband, I agreed. Six fascinating years of teaching followed, before I needed to take up full-time employment, again as a teacher, but in very different circumstances.

~ CHAPTER 10 ~

Writing Stories for Other People
The Babel Fish enters my ear

My Indian Guru, Guptananda, told me he had lived 400 years ago. He showed himself to me in the form of a beautiful picture. In 2001 I had gone incognito to the psychic artist, Patrick Gamble, who paints spirit guides. I arranged the appointment with Patrick via another person and she did not give him any details about me, or the name I am known by. I told him nothing whatever about myself. I sat with Patrick for forty-five minutes while he painted busily and, at the end of the session, he turned the canvas round to show me a very kindly looking guru in typical guru's robes.

Guptananda by Patrick Gamble, psychic artist, 2001

Patrick said, "You already know the guru – this man – don't you? You've been working with him for a while. He showed me piles of papers that you and he have been working on. Lots of writing being done – I don't know why you came to see me; it looks like you know far more about Spirit than I do! "

"No, I really don't," I said, "I feel very ignorant about it all, but yes, the guru is helping me to learn and to teach my classes about yoga philosophy."

I was utterly amazed and delighted. He was spot on! I cannot say that was absolute proof of Divine intervention, because there is room for doubt in this

– my friend could have said something to him, but she has integrity and told me she had said nothing at all. It did feel very special to me, and this picture of Guptananda is reproduced in both my yoga stories books.

A friend heard about my stories; she had contacts in India, where she spent a lot of her time at a big ashram. Some of the devotees were creating a series of books called Sacred and Secular Education in Human Values; one book for each academic school year, starting at five years of age and progressing up to thirteen. They were looking for storywriters and she asked me if I could write for them. I said I could certainly try, thinking that Guptananda might cooperate. He gave me some most beautiful stories, all based in India. They were not specifically about his life, as his yoga stories had been, but were Indian nevertheless. A story called The Flood is one such, and I include it here in this book in Chapter 12. The publisher loved the stories, and asked me if I would be willing to write about people from other countries, because this education scheme was worldwide and needed to reflect people of different nationalities.

I went into meditation and devised a way of getting to a level somewhere out there in the ether, where storytellers in Spirit were available. I had been on many meditative 'journeys', so this did not seem like such an impossible task. When I reached the portal, I would enter, and many figures of white light would be milling around. One would come forward and I would know immediately from their appearance or their voice, where abouts in the world they came from. I greeted them and with my pen in hand, I would write the words that came into my head. The stories all came out perfectly edited, beautifully constructed, and very much to the point. This is in complete distinction from my own efforts in penning this book which has had to be extensively edited.

All I had to do was to provide the spirit guides with subject matter. For the purposes of this education scheme, stories were based on the five Buddhistic values of Love, Peace, Truth, Right action and Non-violence. Those broad subjects were divided into different headings. For example, under the subject of Love would come about ten other headings, such as Kindness, Consideration, Compassion, Gentleness, Forgiveness and so on. It was those headings that were to be the subjects of my stories. As usual I had absolutely nothing in my head before I wrote the stories, but once I had made contact with a spirit guide, the story would flow. This process seems to be a form of telepathy. It was not hard to make contact with my guides. All that was needed was some uninterrupted time by myself, of which I had plenty.

The publisher told me, after all eight books had been created and published, that I was their most prolific story-writer and her favourite. This was a great surprise to me! Never having been a writer and with no ambition to be one, at the time, here I was turning out stories which were being read all over the world. My 'story guides' came from China,

India, Australia, Canada, Alaska, Africa, France, Scotland, England, Ireland, America – and other places I have probably forgotten. The strange thing is that all of these guides spoke perfect English! Perhaps there really is a 'Babel Fish' (put it in your ear and it translates everything) as in Douglas Adams's *Hitchhiker's Guide to the Galaxy*. Maybe someone slipped one into my ear, though I can't say I noticed it happening. This spiritual gift is called clairaudience, which means clear hearing.

I had become a channel for receiving stories and information. I soon discovered that I could ask for guidance in my own life in the same way that I could channel stories. I went through a similar meditation process to make contact with my guides, but did not go to 'Storyland'. Instead, I would ask for help from Spirit, and I would get answers if I listened with a pen in my hand and paper to write on. This was not 'pen-pushed channelling', but more like thought transference at a speed that I could write at – a kind of spiritual dictation. I would ask for advice for myself, and I still do on occasions. The results have always been wise and sensible. They have never surprised me, but confirmed my gut feelings about the issues I needed help with. This has also worked with advice for my sons when they were in their teens and early twenties. I never imposed it on them, it was always just an offering of ideas, and neither of them ever objected. When I started writing this chapter, I began to wonder how they felt about it now, looking back from their forties to their teens. I asked each of them and I will relate their responses here:

My elder son answered me on the phone. In response to my question, he said he was never over-awed by the advice and found it always to be gentle and sensible. It never countered any ideas he had about the way to go and always gave him useful food for thought. He was happy that I had sought the best advice that I could for him, whether it came from 'Spirit', or my 'Higher Self', or even his guardian angel. It is impossible to tell, and I didn't try to elaborate on the source.

My younger son replied in Facebook's Messenger so I can quote his actual words.

"I always appreciated you giving me the time to think about the challenges I might be facing at a particular moment. I also appreciated that you had dedicated some special energy to dig deep to find suggestions for me. Overall, I found the advice 'from Spirit' to be pragmatic, sensible, and entirely in alignment with what I knew of your general views and ethos, so it wasn't surprising or elevated in any way, but did serve as a convenient conduit for me to hear your views, perhaps more explicitly than you felt you could have stated them otherwise. I suppose it formed a way for us to communicate without some of the backlash you might have received whilst cautioning some of my more extravagant behaviours and extreme mindsets! I think your spiritual beliefs have tended to enliven and serve you well over the years. "

I have been asked what came first, the stories or the guidance for myself and others. It is hard to remember exactly what happened 30 years ago, everything happened so fast at first but I believe the guidance came first, for myself at least, and then the stories from Guptananda, after which I realised I could get help for others. I hope that clarifies things a little.

Therapeutic stories
Channelling for others through writing stories for them

I was working on my counselling and psychotherapy diploma while all this writing was going on (1997 -2002) and it occurred to me that stories could be very therapeutic. I asked a social services colleague, who worked in a therapeutic establishment for people with serious mental health troubles, if he knew of a client who might benefit from a story. He was interested in the idea, and had such a client. My objective at the time was to find out if my stories were helpful to counselling clients. I asked the manager to tell me as little as possible about the client, just the main issue that was creating problems for the person. He told me that the client had been abandoned at birth by his twin, who had died in the womb. As a boy growing up, his mother had a section in the freezer for his food, and the rest of the family ate nice freshly cooked food. At that point I asked him to stop immediately. I did not want any more details. That was literally all the information I had of him. I had had no background whatsoever in matters of mental health, or dead twin issues.

I wrote the story which came to me through the customary rapid channel, with no forethought, as usual. The story that came to me was so poignant, tragic and plausible, that I felt brave enough to pass it on to my therapist colleague. I asked him to vet the story to see if it was appropriate for his client. He told me it was uncannily like the young man's story, and entirely appropriate for him. Two months later, on my seeing the manager again, he told me the story had brought about a turning point in the client's life. He was now nearly ready to pass his driving test, was out in the world and looking forward to his future for the first time.

THE STORY — Abandoned at Birth by a twin
Written in 2002 and published in my stories blog: yogastories.co.uk

You may be forgiven for thinking that abandonment by your own twin would mean very little for a person. It is true that for some people who experience this event there is no particular sense of regret or longing. They feel complete in themselves and although they inevitably wonder what their other half would have been like, they go through life in much the same way as any other person who has perhaps lost a brother or sister at birth. There is a little sadness but not much.

For the mother too there is always sadness, always a sense of loss. Some mothers bear it more easily than others. For some there is always a small gap in their lives, a small ache in their hearts. For a few there is a deep longing for the absent person. They may blame the surviving twin in some subconscious way for the death of the other. They may feel that the survivor has been too greedy for life and has taken the life of the other for himself. He may be perceived to have taken too much sustenance from his mother's blood, too much space, too much air, or too much time during the birth. The misguided mother may feel a sense of failure and wish to project the blame of failing to bring two babies into the world on to the one that surives. This usually happens when there are no other brothers or sisters in the family. The mother perhaps had only one chance to produce her children and she failed one of them.

My sister was one such woman. It was very sad. First she had a girl, successfully. There were no difficulties for her. The girl was much loved and treasured, and my sister and her husband hoped for a boy to follow her soon. It was seven long years before she became pregnant again. Such joy! She hoped and prayed for a boy. When she was told she was carrying twins she felt she had been doubly blessed. She would care for them so well. She planned how she would manage her twins. She sought out women who had had twins and discussed it at length with them. She prepared two little cots and two sets of clothes. Everything was ready for her two boys, for this is what she was convinced she had kicking bravely away in her belly.

The time came for her labour. In those days husbands did not attend their wives' delivery. My sister was attended by her doctor and a midwife. Her husband and I waited downstairs. We heard the cries of one baby and then we waited. He paced the floor up and down. Water was fetched, the first baby was welcomed, and we waited. Finally, three hours later, my sister delivered the second twin. He was smaller and blue, she told me, and he was dead.

It was such a strange time. Although they had their longed-for son, they could not be happy because they had lost a child. They were weighed down with their sense of bereavement. No one could convince them otherwise.

The child who survived was very hungry. He cried and sucked and cried and sucked. In my sister's mind this showed her that he had taken the available food from his brother in the womb. She needed someone to blame, as her sense of failure was so great that she could not bear the burden of it alone. She had to share it so she shared it with the surviving twin. Gradually, in her eyes, he became the cause of her loss. Instead of rejoicing in the fact that he had been born and survived, and was strong and healthy, she saw him as a parasite. She knew in her heart that this was not so, but in some twisted turn of mind she relieved herself of her guilt by blaming the living twin. Her husband was drawn in to this way of thinking too. For reasons of his own he colluded with her shame and guilt and was content to put the blame on to the survivor, whom I shall call John.

And what of John? How did all this affect him? As a young baby he became aware of a distance between himself and his parents. They did not hold him and love him in the way that his needful baby heart desired. He cried a lot and only food seemed to comfort him. His sister soon grew impatient with his crying and looked on him as something of a nuisance. He had taken his mother's time and attention from her more than she was prepared to accept. John grew up with a deep sense of aloneness. Something was missing from his life and, as a baby, it felt like a lack of love. When he was old enough to understand, he learnt about his twin, and began to long for him with a deep yearning which, of course, could never be satisfied. His mother's resentment of him became deeply ingrained and he himself felt in some way responsible for her disappointment. He felt apologetic about his own existence. He wished his brother had survived and not himself. He wanted to give up his own life, as it seemed so meaningless, lonely and empty without his 'other half' to share it with. The family took to giving him his own food; it was kept separate and was different from theirs. They felt he ate so much, and was such a good survivor anyway, that he could eat cheap junk food. They needed careful nourishment, as they considered they were more sensitive than he was. He would watch them eat delicious meals while he had to manage on beans on toast or sausages.

Somehow, most of the other relatives had been drawn in to this myth of the greedy, tough twin. They did nothing to change the situation. As John's aunt, I did express my opinion about the unfairness of it all, but I was talked down.

Eventually, fortunately, John met a lovely girl who was able to see through the mistaken thinking and who gave John back his sense of identity. He realised that each person is a separate individual, worthy of love and attention in their own right. Each person has their own path to tread and their own lessons to learn.

I am pleased to say that John now has a family of his own, and each member is loved and appreciated for who they are. I am now a great aunt to one set of twins, and strangely enough to a single survivor of twins. This one is a girl and she was treated with great love and affection from the day she was born. She does sometimes wonder about her dead sister, but does not need her to complete her life.

On July 24th 2014, an item on the BBC radio programme, *Woman's Hour*, was about the difficulties and feelings of parents who lose a twin baby at birth. To me it confirmed why my story above, was so helpful for the survivor twin.

~ CHAPTER 11 ~

On-screen Spiritual Happenings

Publishing my book and blog online for all the world to see

In 1998, quite early on in my new spiritual seeker's life, I had completed the manuscript of the whole book *Guptanada's Stories*. I reached the bottom of the page of the contents list, which was my last task in finishing the book. Each chapter was labelled with a story title and stories numbered one to forty-three. I was debating with myself whether to have a section about me, and about how the book had happened. I did not want to turn the work into an egocentric piece about me as the writer, however, and had almost decided not to include myself. My screen was full of writing all the way to the bottom, each line was a description of the subject matter of the chapter. I completed the acknowledgements line and pressed the 'enter' bar. Another line came up:

"Your Life" it said.

I felt the hairs on my body rising; goose pimples all over. I shouted out in shock and surprise. I had no idea that Spirit could affect the computer. Gerry popped his head round the door.

"What's up?" he asked.

"I've just got a message on my computer screen," I said.

"Well, you are always getting those aren't you?" said Gerry.

"Look. Here. I'd just finished writing out the contents list, and this appeared. It's not an email and I didn't write it. It appeared at the bottom of the page when I pressed enter!" I explained.

"What does it say?"

"'It says 'Your Life'."

"Well, weren't you thinking about writing something about your life?" he said.

"Yes, but I wouldn't have written 'Your Life'. That wouldn't make sense. I would have written 'My Life' because it would be about me."

"Oh yes, you're right," Gerry shrugged. "Well, I don't know, no good asking me."

"No, I'm not asking you, I'm telling you!" I said.

Gerry was completely nonplussed, probably wondering if I had lost my marbles. He didn't argue with me, he just went back to his painting. I've no idea what thoughts were in his head. It's not the sort of thing that most people could possibly believe, which is why I haven't told many people. It did bring to mind a happening in one of Philip Pullman's books, where the computer screen talks to Lyra, the main character. At the time of the 'Your Life' event I was so amazed, delighted and possibly a little frightened, that I wrote to Philip Pullman to ask him if his books were channelled. I wondered if words had appeared on his computer screen too. I had no reply, but recently, in 2019 I think, I heard him in an interview on BBC Radio 4, saying that he thought many writers, including himself, had a spirit or muse that helped to write the stories. Yes! I knew it! They might not have written on his screen of course, but he definitely said a muse was involved in his writing, unless he meant he has a human muse? He also reportedly declares himself to be an atheist. I can understand that. The existence of muses and spirits does not inevitably mean that there is a God, or even gods. That certainty would require a different sort of proof altogether.

Many other writers say the same thing. I remember a radio interview in the mid-nineties with prolific author Isabelle Allende, wife of the ex-president of Chile, who said the spirits of the people in her books come to tell her their stories. I also thought I detected a similar hint from the late Hilary Mantel, the much lauded and awarded British author. It is a slightly difficult thing to tell an audience; one risks losing credibility. Perhaps most writers keep quiet about it until they have sold so many books that it doesn't matter what they say; they have a following of people who will buy their books however the words came to them! Angie Sage, well-known author of many children's books and a friend of our family, told me that she thought most writers were channels. Whether they know it or admit it is another matter!

I began to write stories for other people with problems. It occurred to me that they might have a wider value, and that they should be published. Blogs were a new thing at the time and I decided to create one. The blog was to accompany my yoga stories book, which I published online to make the therapeutic stories available to the world. It became another way of finding people who wanted help and, for me, new subjects to write about. On my blog I suggested that people ask me for stories for free, and they did. There are about 130 stories now available at *yogastories.co.uk*

The blog and the book both went online in 2008. They were very popular and I had nearly half a million visits to each of them in the first years. A number of people wrote and asked if they could use my stories for their own education schemes. That was exactly what I wanted to happen. They are popular in English-speaking countries and nations that have English as a second language, such as in India and the Philippines. Changes to online searches, and the introduction of search-engine optimisation (SEO) have resulted in visits to my blog dwindling. I decided to publish my books as paperbacks and eBooks in order to get the material out to a wider public. I closed down my online book *Guptananda's Stories*, and in 2019 I published my first physical book on the Hindu rules of life, or the *Yamas* and *Niyamas*. It is called, *The Great Little Book of Yoga Stories; Book 1.*

In 2020 I worked on Book 2, *Yoga Stories from Guru Guptananda,* about the Eight Limbs of Yoga, the chakras and the gunas, published in 2022, it is slightly more esoteric and yogic than the rules of life. I found an Indian reader, Abhishek Morye, from among the yoga teachers' community in Cornwall. Abhishek has read my stories and we have produced a lovely audio book to accompany Book 2. At the time of writing I hope we will create an audio book for Book 1 as well.

~ CHAPTER 12 ~

The Flood

One of my favourite channelled stories, written for a world-wide educational scheme

I was asked to write a story about respecting other people's property, under the heading "Right Action". This story came from India, perhaps from Guptananda. It can be found in my blog. It is one of my very favourite stories and came in a year of great floods in Bangladesh.

In my village in India we live very close to the sea. We live in fear of tidal waves, hurricanes, cyclones and even extra-high tides. If the people in my village could have found somewhere else to live, they would have. But most people are too poor to move away, so they stay and pray that the sea will not take them before their time.

When I was about ten years old, we had a terrible flood. I remember it so clearly. The weather had been bad for several days, raining heavily, turning everything into mud. Then we heard there were storms at sea. The tide was very high the night before it happened. My father said we could not risk staying at home for even one more day. He made us pack our belongings and put them into our handcart. My mother readily agreed to go. She was afraid for our lives – the lives of her children, especially the new baby, only three months old. She felt he would be her last child and so he was especially precious to her. There were six of us children altogether, four girls and two boys. Two of my sisters were older than I was and the others had come much later, they were twins and were about three years old.

For me it was quite exciting to pack up all our important things. We did not have very much, but my mother made sure we took our little cooking stove and a large bag of rice along with clothing and bedding and tools for working in the fields. We also took our oil lamp, trying very hard not to break the glass. I wrapped my blanket carefully around it to make sure it was safe.

Many other people had the same idea as us; some had already had water in their homes from the previous night's high tide.

The wind blew and the rain fell and we trudged along the road as soon as it was light enough to see. My father said we must walk at least eight miles to get on to higher ground before the next high tide. This was going to be difficult, but father thought that even if we didn't manage the eight miles at least we would be further inland. Maybe the land would soak up the sea behind us, so that it would not reach us, even if we were still on the low-lying ground.

My elder sisters and I took it in turns to carry the twins. They were very small and could not keep up the pace. Mother carried the baby on her back and helped father to push the cart when he became tired.

After we had been walking for about three hours a terrible thing happened, the wheel fell off our cart. People were streaming past us with their children, animals and all their worldly goods. Everybody's cart was full to the brim. There was no space for our stuff. Mother began to cry as she looked at her little cooker that she loved so much. Would she have to leave it behind?

Time was pressing on. The day was becoming hot and humid and there was still a long way to go. Mother noticed a signpost at the edge of the road. It indicated the way to the next village.

"This is a good marker," she said, and she walked over to a rough brick house. It was open and there were signs that the inhabitants had left hurriedly, leaving little of importance behind them. Mother and Father dragged the cart into the house and draped an old sari she found lying in a corner over it to hide the contents.

"With any luck, when we return, we may find

this house again and reclaim what is ours," she said.

We continued our journey with no food and no water but with our lives intact. We reached the higher ground two hours before the next high tide and storm. The land was devastated. Thousands of houses were washed away and hundreds of lives were lost. Those too old or too ill to make the journey were drowned. Our family was still together – wet, homeless, but together. After five days the local people who had fed us with bowls of rice said we must return to our homelands. There was no room for us in their village. The water had subsided, so return we did. It was difficult to recognise the route we had taken. Dead animals lay strewn everywhere and every so often there was a human corpse. I noticed that several of the dead were people who had a leg or a foot missing – they had not been able to walk fast or far enough.

Father found an old wheel abandoned in the road and was hoping to be able to fix it on to the cart, should we ever find it again. My mother suddenly became excited as she saw in the distance the sign near the brick house where our belongings had been left.

Mother and I ran towards the house. There were some people standing round the door looking tired and dirty. Mother approached them cautiously. She spoke to a man leaning in the doorway. She explained how the cart had broken and she had left it in the hut. She wondered if it was still there.

"Ah, Madam," replied the tired-looking man, "When we returned home all we found was mud, mud, mud. We have not started to clear it away yet. It seems to have half filled our house. Please look for yourself."

Mother looked inside the hut. To her joy she found the leg of the cooking stove poking out through a piece of filthy slime.

"Yes, yes," she exclaimed, "it's there! May we take it?"

"Indeed, Madam, since it is yours. Please feel free to release it from its tomb."

"But what about you? You seem to have nothing left in your house. Are you sure you don't want to keep it? That was the risk we took in leaving it here."

"Madam, I have very little, and neither, I perceive, do you; but what is yours, is yours. Please take it. The Lord will provide for us, unless it is his will that we also should die."

With that the man began to scrape away at the mud. Beneath our cart lay a pile of beautiful cooking pots.

"And these, madam, are these yours too?"
"No," said Mother, "I have never seen these. You must keep them and use them for yourself."
"I will indeed. Until their rightful owner returns, I will consider them to be my own."
He smiled a big smile and his wife looked in wonder at the pots.

On returning to our village we cleared away the mud and resumed our lives. That was ten years ago. I have always remembered that man's understanding of what is mine is mine, what is yours is yours. It is a good way to look at property, and then one will never be tempted to steal it.

QUESTIONS: *Support answers to questions 2 to 7 with evidence from the text.*
1. I have called this story 'The Flood'. What name might you give this story?
2. Why was the village unsafe?
3. Why did the people remain living there?
4. What were the family's most important possessions?
5. What help did they receive from the villagers on the higher ground?
6. What was the attitude of the man who owned the house that had been filled with mud?
7. How did you feel when you heard the story?
8. Did it remind you of anything in your own life?

All my educational stories are followed by questions to make sure the children have understood the message of each story.

~ CHAPTER 13 ~

Sound Mantra

A simple sound leads to a wonderful, uplifting message that keeps me positive for years

One summer, probably 1998, I was invited to go to a special mantra (chanting) evening in a large hall over a clubhouse in Bodmin, Cornwall. I was used to the idea of mantras because they are part of the yogic tradition, but they had never done much for me. As I had a lot of respect for the lady who invited me, I went along. The instructor, Ken Mellor, was a well-known practitioner in mantra meditation, who had come over from Australia to share his experience and knowledge with us in the UK. The forty people who were gathered spread themselves out around the hall; there was plenty of space for everybody. We could choose to sit on the floor or on a chair.

"The mantra is OM TAT SAT, which in translation means roughly I AM THAT. In other words we are recognising our own individual divinity," said the teacher. "The meditation will last about twenty minutes. We will start by relaxing and then we'll get on to the mantra. You will be saying – speaking rather than singing – OM TAT SAT together out loud for five minutes. Then you will whisper it together for five minutes, followed by five minutes of mouthing it silently. Then finally you have to say it internally, making no sound or lip movements."

The instructor told us he would put on some background music. We made a start with the relaxation. Very soon after that a loud, fairly raucous sound surrounded us. I thought to myself that this was very avant-garde for a meditation. It had a strong pulse and felt more like 'heavy metal'. However, I felt myself being drawn in to the meditation and ceased to wonder about the music. The teacher came round and touched us all on the centre of our foreheads. After a couple of minutes a different sort of music superimposed itself over the heavy beat. I later discovered that the first music was from a clubroom beneath the room we were in! But it didn't matter at all, the sound, whatever it was, carried us along with the mantra. At some point I felt myself surrounded by a strong energy field. It felt warm and seemed to have a physical density, almost like cotton wool, all around me. My arms, which were resting on my thighs, felt as if they were floating, supported by the energy force. I felt a triangle of energy, which I could perceive as light, coming from my third eye in the middle of my forehead, and extending to each hand. I had started the meditation weighed down with paralysing worries concerning my life, my growing incompatibility with my husband. Towards the end of the meditation, I had a vivid vision of four different scenes that came with words, I could see them all clearly, one by one, along with the words that came with them. It was almost like an illustrated poem.

"You are nothing more than a grain of sand in the desert.

You are nothing more than a drop of rain in the ocean.

You are nothing more than a leaf in a forest.

You are nothing more than a snowflake on a mountaintop."

It was so dramatic, so beautiful and so surprising that it took away all my everyday concerns and put them into perspective. It was very uplifting. The healing effect of this event lasted a long time. I was so grateful for having experienced it.

I have since tried to replicate this mantra experience, both by myself and with my own meditation groups, but nothing in particular has happened, except for some moments of clarity when I was painting a large and difficult picture, but I will explain that later.

~ CHAPTER 14 ~

The End of an Era

We leave our country cottage

The mantra meditation gives a clue about the trajectory of my life. Things were slowly falling apart, and the vision I received strengthened my resolve to continue on my path in as positive a way as possible. I needed to update my computer skills to become employable and Gerry needed more time and inspiration to paint.

The situation had become untenable in our lovely cottage. We could no longer afford the mortgage, and we were both utterly stressed out. G's paintings were showing that his heart was not in them, and I couldn't squeeze any more yoga or keep-fit classes into my schedule to earn more money. I felt so distressed about the shaky state of our relationship, and having to leave our home, that I asked a local man who was a healer to come and give me some healing. It made a huge difference to me. He simply placed his hands on my head while we sat in our beautiful garden, surrounded by flowers. After about fifteen minutes, I felt very different. I was able to face the future with equanimity. Suddenly I could think straight again, and although nothing had outwardly changed in our situation, I felt a great weight had been taken away from me. So interesting, looking back – the healer in me could not heal myself at that time, but another healer could. I got on and organised the sale of our house and field. We bought a smaller place in our local village, staying connected to our friends and activities.

About a month after the move I discovered I had breast cancer. I was forty-eight. I learnt that all of the women in my cancer support group at the hospital had suffered a great deal of stress shortly before their cancer manifested. That was in 1999 when the relationship between cancer and stress was not recognised by the medical profession.

My cancer was small and the radiotherapy treatment only lasted six weeks after the lump was excised. Normally I avoid taking medicines and the chemotherapy that they offered me, in pill form, did not appeal at all. I had a very strong intuitive sense that I did not need the chemo. Twenty-five years have gone by and I now know I was right, for me at least.

My dear friend , artist Alan Nisbet drew the picture below for me after my cancer diagnosis. He designed it to encourage me to be positive about my life and my state of health. He included all the important elements in my life that kept me interested and keen to get on with living an exciting, healthy and wonderous life. The symbology is very clear to me, and is very personal. Alan illustrated my first two books of yoga stories and my fourth book about

Native American lore, currently only present on my yogastories blog, but which I hope to publish next.

Gerry and I did everything we could to make the best of our new life. G left the male voice choir he had sung with and conducted on and off for twenty years. He started up a mixed group in our sitting room, so that at long last I could be part of the choir he was running. Very soon the choir became too large and migrated across the road to the village pub. We helped to set up a samba band, run by our younger son, in the local village hall and an improvisation drama group that performed around the local villages twice a year. There was a lot of fun, but also a strong undercurrent of angst in our lives.

Then my mother came to live with us. Looking after a parent is a time to be treasured, so people say, but when it is actually happening, it can be very difficult indeed. For me, a major part of the issue was never knowing how long it was going to go on for. There were wonderful moments of sharing and appreciation, no doubt about that. We drove round the Cornish lanes for two spring seasons, loving the daffodils, primroses and bluebells. We shared memories and explained things that had been taboo in earlier times. Mother always thought she'd be 'going back home soon' to her house in Ipswich and I had to learn how to deal with that. She was always a gentle soul, and this part of her personality shone through right till the end.

Mother passed away after eighteen months in our care. Suddenly it was just Gerry and me staring at each other and wondering how on Earth we could make our relationship work. Using some of my inheritance money we were able to go abroad and visit all our relatives at different times over the next couple of years. We went to Australia, New Zealand, Cyprus and Ireland. We even went to Greece, where there were no relatives – the idea of going to the Greek islands appealed to both of us. The experience was delightful in many ways – the nightingales, scops owls and magical olive groves, but sadly, we just could not share the joy. Spending months in close proximity in a campervan accompanied by someone that one can't communicate with any more is not to be recommended. We had come to a grinding halt. Marriage guidance did not help. We both saw that we needed to go our separate ways. And that's what we did after thirty years of married life. I felt a strange mixture of exhilaration and freedom and a huge sense of grief and loss. Lost dreams. Lost friends. Lost home.

This is not part of my life that I choose to share in detail with the world. The time to part had come and we separated amicably. I attended computer training to enable me to enter the world of work and earn a living. I moved from my house in a village on the fringe of Bodmin Moor into a Victorian terrace in a small town ten miles away from the moor. I found the perfect job, teaching horticulture to special needs teenagers at the local college of further education. There were a lot of other subjects on the curriculum and I found myself teaching all sorts of other things as well. It was a great joy, and brought together all the skills I had acquired over my fifty-three years.

If angels were at work for me then, and somebody had told me that was definitely the case, I would have believed them. The first time I opened a local newspaper and looked in the jobs section. there was my perfect job. No further searching required. With this new job there was no time for writing or healing, as the demands of the work were considerable, but being something of a Mrs Fix-It, I would always offer healing to friends if they seemed to need it and were open to the idea of it. If nothing else, a healing session always provided a gentle, relaxing time, which might well be all that was needed. The mystical side continued to be part of my new life and my knowledge of relaxation and recharging helped me to cope with the heavy demands of my new teaching career.

~ CHAPTER 15 ~

Teaching in the College of Further Education

Dreams, energy zaps and visual messages

When we are on a path in life that recognises spirituality, we may find that we get dreams that are highly relevant to our situation. Such dreams can provide significant lessons. I have had a number of these dreams. Early on in my new career I had a vivid dream. I saw myself choking on and spitting out pink paper, yellow paper and green paper. I felt that I was suffocating in paper. This was a clear reflection of one of the aspects of the job that none of us teachers appreciated. It was the excessive recording of every element learnt by every student on every subject. In my opinion it was ridiculous, and the dream inspired me to write about all this unnecessary paperwork to the principal of the college, incognito, I have to admit! I put up with it because I was having such fun teaching the kids. Over the years I taught gardening, floristry, cooking, woodwork, art, music appreciation, numeracy, literacy, dance, personal care, hygiene in the home, and all at a level that the students and I could cope with. It was called 'Entry Level'. No preliminary skills were needed from the students, except the ability to sit and participate at the level each student was capable of. We had a great team of staff and a happy department.

I continued to teach yoga, both to the students and to the staff – we had a class for the teachers once a week. The students included some with Down's syndrome and others with various disabilities. They all loved the yoga and particularly enjoyed the relaxation and meditation that we did. I would always talk them through a beautiful scene, so their minds held a picture of places such as a gorgeous beach in the moonlight or a cool glade in a wood. I kept the visualisations simple for them, but my own meditations were sometimes more nuanced and specific, when I was feeling unsure and was looking for answers.

I tried a different type of meditation when I was trying to decide if I should marry my second partner. He was so very different from the first, and I was about 95% sure it would be a good thing to do. I went to a beautiful wood in the valley of the River Fowey, when the bluebells were out in all their glory. I decided to ask a lovely big oak tree for advice, through meditation (never having talked to trees before, but knowing that some people do!). I sat beneath it and leaned against its rough bark, surrounded by a sea of blue bells. The oak seemed to tell me that trees have no choice where they grow, they just put down roots and make the very best of their situation. 'Be Like the Trees', it said. In my case this was very good advice, and I went ahead. We had a number of very happy years together. I don't make a habit of asking trees for advice, relying more on angelic forces which seem to be more accessible and which go into some detail when I am channelling them. On this occasion I was pleased with the short communication that said so much.

I re-married, but after a few years my second husband, Bryn, became quite poorly and decided to retire. It was such a good decision for him. He too was teaching at the college, and had been finding the paperwork irksome. I was able to support him with my earnings, so he had time to tinker with his vintage car and chat with his buddies on the allotment. At this time a strange phenomenon started to happen to me. When I was lying down in bed at night I started to hear a loud sound in my head.

'*Sshhhuuup*', is the only way I can describe it, and it was accompanied by a crack of electricity, which felt like a jolt. These 'zaps' would usually happen about three times and then I could go to sleep. I didn't understand it at all. It usually started at my head and went straight down my spine. Sometimes it went in the other direction. It could be very noisy and jolting. I went to see my doctor who had never heard of any such thing, but was able to comfort me by saying that it was not the symptom of any ailment that he knew about. I had a suspicion that it might have to do with my energy meditations –

when I pictured coloured light entering my body with each breath and recharging my chakras. This is something that I did every day and had done for years. It always made me feel replenished. People who know something about yoga, I figured, might be able to give me an answer. I put my question on something called Ask.com online. An Indian doctor replied. He told me it was Kundalini energy, something yogis understand, and was nothing to worry about. I came to see it as a healing element in my life. My husband was growing progressively more poorly. He was always able to carry out everything he wanted to do without any problems, but with diminished energy. My own energy zaps increased in number. I decided to go to an ashram in Wales, recommended by a yoga friend, to see if they could shed any light on the phenomenon.

During my stay at the Mandala Yoga Ashram, I was required to work hard, doing 'seva' or 'service to God'. This involved doing chores every day, such as cleaning or cooking. It was a delightful place and a joy to be there. We had daily yoga practice and meditation. I met a man there who was experiencing the same as me, and was not at all worried about it. That was a comfort. I had no zaps while I was in Wales, or for a week after my little break away. Then, seven days after my stay, I was woken by a whole series of zaps that went on and on, repeating about every twelve seconds. This carried on for hours. At first I thought I would welcome it, if it was healing whatever needed to be healed, and then

I tired of it. It kept waking me up and shaking me up. I pleaded for it to stop and eventually it did stop. I will never know what it really meant. I never experienced anything like that again, but I've often had two or three zaps before going to sleep. Many years later, long after the passing of my second husband, I occasionally get a zap, and it feels like a welcome friend. Sometimes I think it came to give me strength to cope with Bryn's illness and death. Whatever it was I may never know.

At the same time as the period when I was having energy zaps, and only on one occasion, a strange thing happened. I was lying in bed and I heard three trumpet-like blasts of the most astonishing, amazing and delightful sounds in my head. It was not external. It was so wonderful that I yearned for years to hear it again. I have heard about 'the music of the spheres' and those three notes seemed to be of that ilk. But at the time of writing I don't think I'm ready to join the heavenly choir yet.

I have had very few frightening experiences. Our teacher in the meditation circle told us that we are protected by our own goodness. She taught us to refuse to entertain negative energies.

"Tell them to go away," she said. "You are in charge. Don't let them create fear in you, because that's what they feed off. Surround yourself in love and light. Call upon your deity, or Archangel Michael, a great protecting Angel, if you are troubled by negative things."

I occasionally saw an inner vision of ugly faces

peering at me curiously when I was relaxing, just before going to sleep. I told them to go away and they went. On one occasion I was asleep, lying on my front, and was woken by something that felt like a 'cat-dragon' on my back. It felt heavy and horrible. I could 'see' it but not with my eyes. In my mind I surrounded myself with love and light and called out to Jesus and the Lord God Almighty. It didn't stay for long, quickly disappearing. It never returned. I told Bryn about it in the morning, and he told me of a rather similar time when, one night, a large ugly creature, presumably not from the earthly realm, had jumped on to his chest, and he'd had to physically wrestle with it to get rid of it.

These experiences were frightening for both of us, but we were each able to defend ourselves in our own way. We would never know if it had just been a dream, but at least we had a way of dealing with such things. My teacher had told us that when we first begin to open up to Spirit, we shine a light that may attract attention from negative entities. They are curious and they may come to have a look, but when they realise that the newly illuminated 'light person' has no interest in them and no fear, they go away and don't return. Yes, I too thought it was all a bit far-fetched. At least it equipped me with the tools to deal with that situation should it arise. It did arise and I was okay.

Because of my upbringing as a Catholic I would always turn to Jesus in times of trouble, but I'm confident that people who have other deities are equally protected, guided and loved. I believe all deities are representatives of the Source, Universal Energy, or God

~ CHAPTER 16 ~

Psychometry and Visions

*Starting my own meditation
group at home*

A year after Bryn's sad passing from this world in 2010, I was very lucky to meet David. Living alone did not suit me at all, neither did it suit David who had also lost his partner the previous year.

My home with David, whom I married in 2014, is a haven for retirement, where I can do lots of gardening and as much spiritual activity as I want. David has a doctorate in science. He is another sceptic, but he has made good progress towards understanding where 'I am coming from' spiritually speaking. This is fortunate as otherwise he might have come to think he had married a 'nutter'. He had, in fact, put me on the 'rejects list' of possible partners on the dating website we were using, because of my spiritual interests. However, he liked the photos of me and my emails, and when we met his initial opinion changed rapidly.

In our early years together I made a big effort to get to know people in the local town. We started a meditation circle in our home, with people I knew well enough to be happy that we could create a lovely positive atmosphere. David always came along too. With the log fire and the dim lights he would usually fall asleep during meditation, but he would listen while everyone reported their meditational experiences. Most of us had already attended the meditation circle of a very spiritual lady in our local town. She had introduced us to a number of deities, such as Quan Yin and Thoth, in her meditation sessions. When she closed her circle, I wanted to start one myself.

I had no background knowledge of different deities, but I felt I had other things to offer our own group at home. We often had visiting speakers who were able to demonstrate a variety of skills. Something that fascinated me was the practice of psychometry. One way of doing this, is to hold an item belonging to one of the group of meditators, previously supplied, then discretetly placed in a box. Each person would then choose an object from the box, meditate upon it and see what came to mind. We tried this with our group. The results were fascinating. Everyone picked up some information relevant to the owner of the item. What came through was a vignette of a story that was very meaningful to the owner of the object. It seems there is a spiritual link between the object and the owner, which can be divined by the meditator.

On one of these occasions, we experimented to see if the vibrations of a person could be transferred to a simple piece of paper with a number on it. I gave one to everybody and they meditated while holding it in their hands, imprinting the paper with their 'vibe'. Each participant then put the paper into a hat. We all took out the first piece of paper that came to hand and meditated on it. The results were quite startling for some of us. Information that nobody else knew came from those pieces of paper. The person meditating upon the piece of paper just delivered the message to the whole room. The 'owner' of the paper knew their number, and was in every case able to interpret the message or vision. The information was both specific and accurate. In one case it was so intimately personal to the lady whose number had been chosen, that she could not speak about it to the group, except to say that it was all relevant and correct and too personal to share. She could tell me only afterwards what it meant to her. It was a very big issue, about a family secret recently revealed to her; the name of the family member involved and a one-word encapsulation of the event came across during the psychometry. The event in question had changed the lives of all families involved in this discovery, when it had occurred several years previously. It was an example of adoption information coming to the fore. I think that the importance of this revelation by Spirit was to help this lady understand that there are in reality other realms that can impinge upon our human realm.

From my point of view it could be helpful for us all to understand more clearly that we do have angels and helpers – often the spirits of those who have gone before – watching over us. I think over the years it has been demonstrated to my husband David and other sceptics in our group that other realms do indeed exist and that we have a choice whether we pay attention to this information or not. My purpose in enabling and encouraging such activities is to confirm to participants that these realms exist and do have a bearing on our lives, and that further study and meditation might reveal helpful advice for us in our Earth-bound lives.

Visions
Occasionally I have been given visions. I had always thought of them as being of a religious nature, like those of St Bernadette at Lourdes and her visions of the Virgin Mary, mother of Jesus Christ. The ones I have had were nothing of that sort. They have been amusing or puzzling, or both, and always very relevant to my life at the time. Visions have a purpose; they are one way in which Spirit can speak to us without using words. The visions I have had may be compared to a picture or brief video, they are very vivid and clear, but short lived.

I usually have my visions on waking up. I haven't had very many. One was of myself and David, our arms stretched out, pegged onto the washing line. I, in particular, seemed to be stuck there – I couldn't get off it. I didn't understand the meaning at all. The next day I kept asking myself, *What was I doing on the washing line? What was I doing stuck on the washing line? What was I doing stuck on a line?* Then came the 'aha' moment. I had been spending far too much time 'online', on social media or watching time-wasting videos of cute animals being saved or of dog-training for badly behaved pooches, and so on. I was frittering away valuable time. After retirement every year is a bonus. That vision spurred me on to create my first paperback book—'The Great Little Book of Yoga Stories' from my collection of Guptananda's stories.

Visions seem to represent an answer to a problem in unusual ways that you yourself would not ever have thought of. They say or show something in a totally original way. I think mine of the washing line illustrated that really well. That's what makes visions so unique and convincing.

Another vision that I remember very clearly, was of a similar sort to the washing-line image. I was being presented with a gold starfish on a blue velvet cushion. Strangely enough I knew exactly what that meant. It came when I was spending a great deal of time working either in the garden or in the house, cooking and cleaning. I was feeling frustrated and rather unsatisfied.

There is a story in spiritual circles that says every person is allocated a bucket of fish. The fish represent our gifts and talents. If we don't use our fish they decay and rot, we won't be able to use them at all. We will have to throw them away. I was not employing the talents and gifts that I have been blessed with and that I love to use. I can write, draw, paint and sing. Those are my gifts, and I wasn't using them. Rather I was trying to please my husband

and work very hard in the garden, because he is always working hard. This starfish represented my gifts. The message was; *You will never be a star, but you do have gifts. You should use them or you will lose them, then you will feel frustrated and disappointed*' How I agreed with that vision! It gave me the impetus to explain my feelings to David. He immediately accepted what I was saying, and we decided to employ a gardener twice a week to help temporarily with our large garden. I, meanwhile, painted a beautiful big picture of one of our flowerbeds, designed with Van Gogh in mind – only blue and yellow flowers allowed. Creating the picture was such great pleasure and joy. It was only the second large picture I had ever painted, at 80cm x 40cm, and I was thrilled with the result.

A vision came to me when I was waiting for a friend to have a healing session at The Healing Tree, in Cornwall. Derek Gane has created a lovely healing centre on land just outside Launceston. He had recently constructed a stone labyrinth. I walked around it, then I went to sit and meditate nearby. A wolf 'came' to me. It came up close so that I could see its face and shoulders clearly. It was shaggier than a wolf, like a hairy, wolf-like Alsatian dog. After a while Derek came to say they had finished the session and to ask how I got on in the area. I told him about walking his new labyrinth, and my vision of a wolf, and I said I wasn't sure about its identity; it could have been a dog.

Derek's dog called Tara, or 'Wolf'

He told me that a year previously he had buried his treasured old dog, 'Wolf', a German shepherd, just at the edge of the labyrinth. Someone who considers themself psychic would have taken that as par for the course. Being me, and not too sure yet of my gifts, I was very surprised and delighted that this had happened.

To me it was proof of some sort of spiritual input, but I understand that others may not be convinced of the spiritual nature of those visions. They could say the vision of the wolf was the product of my subconscious mind, or some sort of psychic ability, whatever that is. My question is, how did that part of me know about the old dog?

My final vision to date happened on the first day of the first pandemic lockdown in the UK. March 23rd 2020. On waking I saw a clear picture of Mother Earth distraught and angry with the human race. She was shaking and trembling and throwing people off her surface. The people were being scooped up by angels. This was at a time in 2019 and 2020 when forest fires were raging in many hot areas of the world. Tornadoes, hurricanes and tidal waves were battering the lands and shores of many countries. Then a wave of Corona Virus swept across the world. I just had to paint this vision. It took me a month of work. It was very challenging. It was big–nearly two feet by three feet, or 60cm x 84 cm. On two occasions I really didn't know how to progress. I was attending a mantra class at the time, however, and after chanting the mantras my painting solutions came to me instantly and I was able to continue the work.

Crystal healing and visions

A member of my meditation group was learning to become a crystal healer and asked me if I would be a subject for her to practise on. I don't seem to have much affinity with crystals, but I agreed as I find all healing modalities interesting.

During the session I saw the Pope beside me, participating in my healing. He waved his hand over me and said *'You are forgiven for leaving the Church, you don't need to be a Catholic to be a good person'*. I loved that vision. Leaving the Church had always been a subject of doubt and sadness in me. The very next day on Facebook there was a picture of the Pope and he was declaring to the world the same message: "You don't need to be a Christian to be a good person." Crystal healing showed me yet another aspect of opening up to the spiritual side of life via a different route. Each time I have had a crystal healing session, a revelation or significant memory has come to me and helped me along my path. This has happened at least three times.

Seeing a spirit in my bedroom
My late husband, Bryn, appeared to me by my bedside as an instantly recognisable silhouette, at three o'clock one morning in August 2022. He had died in hospital twelve years previously, five days after heart surgery, in 2010.

During his illness, Bryn had a lovely lady doctor, whom I had never met. He used to talk about her and recount the fun conversations he had with her. I knew her name and was thrilled when I met her for the first time in the town where I now live, in 2023. She had recently moved here. I was serving at our local plant swap, and had a good chat with her about plants. Then, not knowing her, I thought to ask her name. Slowly the cogs started turning in my brain, her unusual name rang a bell, though it took a few hours to realize who she was. I was so excited to think that this was actually Bryn's doctor, and that I would be able to talk to her about him and the fascinating and amusing stories he used to share with anyone he thought might appreciate them. That night he appeared to me as a grey shadow, his profile so clearly defined, it was Bryn without a doubt. I sat up and tested to see if my eyes were open. They were, and it was clearly him. He leaned towards me and I whispered his name, then he was gone.

I have not 'seen' him since, though he was 'seen' by a medium a few years ago. Bryn appeared to her as a boxer, in his red boxers' shorts, grinning. The medium was a bit flummoxed because I am what some people regard as 'a bit posh' and not perhaps the sort to be married to a boxer. But Bryn was a champion featherweight boxer while he was in the Royal Navy! He had been a very tiny baby, weighing less than one kilogram, so when he was a lad his father had encouraged him to put on some muscle and learn to defend himself by boxing. It worked!

I understand that spirits appear to their loved ones when those on earth are strongly thinking about them, perhaps at anniversaries, birthdays, holiday times and so on. In my case it was his doctor who caused the strong energetic and emotional connection for me. Bryn must have felt it and been drawn to me from his mysterious and incomprehensible place in heaven.

~ CHAPTER 17 ~

Quan Yin

A goddess comes into my life, unbidden, bringing comfort and help

I hadn't realised how my own health issue, an arthritic hip, had led me to an introduction to the Goddess Quan Yin, until I started to write about my brother's illness.

My middle brother P left the UK to study for an MSc in France. He met and married a French girl and lived the whole of the rest of his life in southern France. It expanded his lifestyle. He would go windsurfing in summer and skiing in winter. His facility with languages enabled him to become a translator of students' work at the University of Toulouse. Every science student had to produce a final dissertation written in both French and English on the subject they happened to be studying. My brother, being a scientist and a French speaker, and a very friendly and willing helper, took on the correcting of translations. He did this initially as a favour, and very soon as a way of earning extra money. After he completed his MSc, he was officially employed by the university both to teach English to the French students and to translate dissertations.

The wine, the food, the socialising all suited my brother's character very well. He had become a smoker as a young man and he was completely hooked on tobacco. He was only forty-two when his first wife died and they had no offspring together. He and his second wife had two children. He was always laughing and joking and was very much involved in his children's lives, but as they approached their teenage years he developed emphysema, a disease of the lungs brought on by many years of smoking. This began to severely restrict his physical participation in family life. Within ten years, although he could continue his translating business from home, he could hardly cross the room as his lungs were so damaged. It came to the point when he decided that he would risk having a lung transplant, he could not continue life as it was.

Meanwhile I was suffering from arthritis in my hip. I tried every alternative treatment available to me rather than go for a hip replacement. Finally, I did have my hip joint replaced and it has been a great success. One of the therapies I tried before that was called Bowen technique. The practitioner said it was very like energy healing, or spiritual healing. I had two sessions. During the second session, in my mind's eye, I saw a Chinese or Japanese woman kneeling beside me and apparently adding to the healing energy that was coming via my therapist.

After the session I asked him about the apparition that I had seen. He told me that his wife was an ardent follower of Quan Yin, who is eternal protector of women and children according to Buddhist religion', and is the main goddess of Chinese people. She is considered to be a bodhisattva – a person who has lived on Earth and whose existence, after death, is dedicated to healing and comforting people on the Earth plane. I knew about Quan Yin, as one of my teachers in meditation circle had introduced us to her and in our meditation we had opened ourselves up to her wonderful, compassionate energy.

I wanted to try to enlist her help, if indeed she had any help to give, to heal my dear brother.

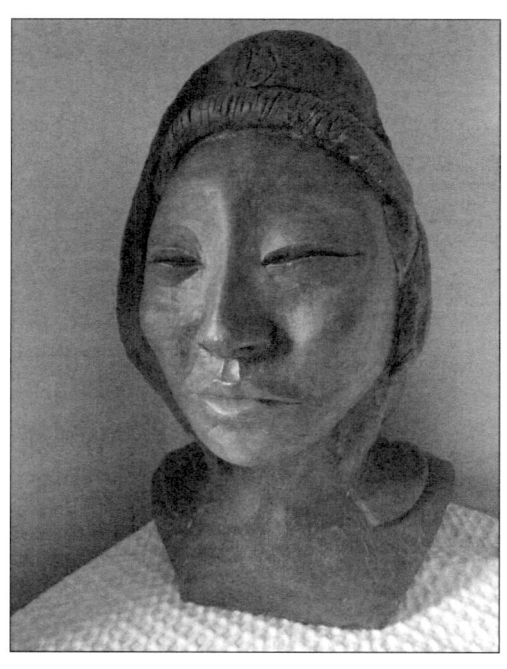

First of all my younger son and I made a statue, the head and shoulders of Quan Yin, and from that statue, my husband and I created concrete busts of the goddess. We placed one in the garden, and one in our wood among the bluebells in a lovely dell bordered by a stream. Every day I walked through the dell, chanting a mantra to Quan Yin, asking for her intervention to help my brother.

I thought I would try some channelled drawing to see if I could contact Quan Yin that way. To my delight the pen moved on paper and a charming and surprisingly constructed face was drawn, not in a way that any artist would draw a face. Although I could not understand the words that came with the drawing, I loved the sweetness of the portrait of her.

I continued my chanting, encouraged by the drawing, but my brother's health continued to deteriorate. He was waiting to make a decision about accepting a transplant. I went for another drawing, and this time the pen made some strange feather like shapes, all coming from one side of the sheet of paper, and then finally another picture of Quan Yin appeared. I kept the pen on the paper and asked what the feathery shapes were about. The following words appeared, all joined up of course, as that's how my channelled writing appears. I have separated out and punctuated the words here:

Quan Yin greets you, disciple. These are my winds that blow me to where I am called
OM Quan Yin

I was overjoyed, and over-awed!

*Quan Yin with sacred winds; a photo
of the drawing that came to me*

To me this was another definite proof that other planes exist. I loved the fact that the word 'disciple' appeared – I would never have thought of calling myself a 'disciple', but more of a respectful, pleading supplicant. I thought a 'disciple' would need to have studied and followed a god or goddess for some time. With regard to the winds, I looked up 'Quan Yin winds' on Google search and I found reference to Quan Yin's sacred winds. I had certainly never heard of them before.

My brother meanwhile agreed to the transplant, and within two weeks a suitable donor had been found. This felt like very good news, although not for the poor donor, a young man who died in a motor-cycle accident. This story does not have a happy ending. My lovely, funny, wonderful brother died within a month of the operation. The new lung never seemed to work properly. However, when I consider the suffering he might have undergone, I felt that Fate had decreed his future and that Quan Yin would have helped in any way that she could. My dear brother died in 2016, at the age of sixty three. Quan Yin has a place in our dell whenever she needs to relax and be at peace. Perhaps her compassion has made me more compassionate towards others in my life. I hope so!

~ CHAPTER 18 ~

Guidance and messages

Meditation can lead to very wise words for the meditator or for their clients

One of the advantages of being a channeller is that one can access written guidance for oneself as well as for others. While I am reticent about giving advice to others, I have used my ability to tap into my own higher guidance on many occasions when I have been searching for answers in my own life. I have found the guidance always to have been clear, concise and eminently sensible. It has given me the courage to go ahead when I have had my doubts. There is never any feeling of imposition, no 'oughts', and nothing has turned out to have been 'poor guidance'.

On one rare occasion I was asked to meditate for a client (who had M.E). She suffered quite debilitating periods of very low energy. In my meditation, I saw an elderly woman who called herself 'Lil'.

"That's my grandma!" said my client.

"She's telling me your illness is because of your father's attitude," I told her.

"Grandma was actually called Adeline," the client explained, "but we all called her 'Fag-Ash Lil'; she always had a fag hanging out of her mouth. She was Dad's mother. I think she's right. I was born before the war and then my father disappeared for the whole of the war. When he came back I was five. He had some definite ideas of how I should be, and I was not whatever he was hoping for, or expecting. I could never ever please him. My sister was born five years after me and in my father's eyes she could never do any wrong. I know I'm a perfectionist and a people-pleaser, but nothing is ever quite good enough. I wear myself out. I know I do."

I hope my client was able to address this tendency, and see it for what it was – a reaction to her father's unreasonable demands, and not a behaviour set in stone!

Kathy's story

The following story also illustrates how spirit can helpfully reveal itself. On meeting David, who three years later became my third husband, many joys came my way; a bluebell wood with a gorgeous dell and a meditation seat were amongst them. Another joy was meeting his interesting friends, in particular Kathy. I had never met such an impressive lady before. She invited us to one of her parties that she held in her centuries old and intriguing Cornish cottage in a tiny hamlet on the edge of Bodmin Moor.

Kathy had spent her working life as a teacher and served as National President of a teacher's union. A warm and welcoming person, she has a huge circle of friends, many of them pagan like herself. Her parties were held in celebration of important traditional festivals such as 'Crying the Neck' – a celebration of the successful bringing in of the harvest in September. Another, 'Wassailing' is done in January to bless the apple trees and to ask for a good crop in the autumn. Birthdays and Christmas are often celebrated too. There is always music and singing at Kathy's parties and traditional mumming occurs around Twelfth Night, where an ancient play is enacted, depicting the triumph of good over evil – when St George kills the Dragon. Kathy is a great singer, writer and a Cornish Bard. The house is filled with fascinating people on these occasions, who join Kathy with their songs and their instruments, their stories and their sense of fun. Many of them bring a plate of delicious food to add to the already groaning table. K is a master cook – this is her forté. Every year she produces jams, jellies pickles and fortified spirits such as sloe gin. She bakes cakes, tarts, scones, buns and many other delicacies for her legendary parties. This, I believe, has been her Achilles heel. Her food is so very tasty and appealing and her gatherings so frequent that she has a serious weight problem. She retired from work early because of weight related issues.

She had told me about the covenant on the house. It was a very unusual condition of sale. The deeds say twice a year she has to provide cakes or bread and ale to the workers on the manorial farms, so she combines this obligation with the 'Crying the Neck' and the Wassail events, bringing in people, music, singing, food and joy. She readily acquiesced to this condition, surprising as it was, because those are the very things that she most values in her life – fellowship, good food, celebration and song.

One day I was meditating in my seat in the bluebell wood and it came to me that I should ask Kathy if she would like to have a session of healing with me. She was going through another bout of illness. I felt quite reticent about asking her, as she might have been offended, I didn't know her very well at that point, but she was very open to this idea. During the healing session in Kathy's dining room, I felt the presence of a spirit. Kathy had told me that spirits lived in the house with her and that they were benign – a comforting presence, so I wasn't surprised or frightened. This apparition was a woman in a simple, long green gown, she was between 40 and 50 years old and she was weeping. She told me she thought that Kathy's health problems were partly her fault. She was very contrite, sorry that Kathy was suffering in this way. The conditions that she had imposed on the sale of the house several centuries previously had had unforeseen circumstances on this Kathy, her latest tenant. The spirit told me her name was Lilibet. A great sadness came over me. It was hard for me not to weep myself. Lilibet faded and I completed the healing session and reported to Kathy what had been revealed.

Of course, I could have created this story either consciously or unconsciously knowing about the covenant on the house, but I had absolutely no idea that the name Lilibet would resonate with Kathy. It turned out that on the deeds of the house, the first owner, who was the Lady of the Manor, was called Elizabeth Charke. The house had been built for her on the death of her husband. Kathy was fascinated to think that Lilibet should appear and take part of the blame for her illnesses. She readily accepted that idea and wondered what she could do for herself to deal with the problem.

Kathy carries on with her parties, dutifully and enjoyably creating marvellous events for her many friends. Her health improves and she tackles great works in the garden with her chickens and cats. Then she has a relapse and needs to rest and recover. In recent years she announced that she had taken a new job – that of a 'Cat Cuddler', her official new title. She has been travelling 20 miles twice a week to a cat rescue centre, to give cuddles and attention to needy cats. She has written and published a book about the farm cat next door who continually tries, and fails, to move in. Her oldest cat is twenty two, evidence that not only the spirits are happy in her welcoming house, but so are the cats!. Kathy's book 'Charlie, Tales of a Cornish Farm Cat' is available on Amazon.

Once, guidance came to me in the form of a poem. It was at a time when I was struggling in my first marriage. I was in my car, just parking it to go shopping, and the poem came into my head. This had never happened before and hasn't happened since but there it was, and it made such sense to me, and altered my behaviour and way of thinking. It seemed so appropriate for so many people that I would often hand it out to my yoga class members. I even went to a calligraphy class for a year, to learn how to produce a nicely scripted version of the poem. At that time, in the late nineties, I had no computer skills at all, and there were no calligraphic fonts on computers anyway! Here it is in modern calligraphy. Think about it!

Live in the Now

Live in the Now my dear, Live in the Now,
Enjoy each precious moment as it passes.
Feel the sun on your face, feel it warming your skin,
Feel the rain on your brow and the wind in your hair.
Do not spend your time in the 'What might have been'
Nor in thinking about 'What probably never will be',
But treasure the moment, for in truth
All we ever have is Now.

~ CHAPTER 19 ~

Conclusion to Part One

I hope you have enjoyed reading my book so far! I felt it was time to explain why I believe what I believe, both to those people who have some belief in other realms, and to those who have said that they thought my work was 'poppycock'. Actually it was only one person, reporting on her son's opinion. Of course there are plenty of sceptics around. Perhaps many of them would not even consider reading a book such as this because their minds are completely closed to spiritual things. I am encouraged by the fact that my previously rather sceptical husband David now says that he is very comforted by what he has witnessed during our meditation circles. He feels there appears to be something beyond what science can, at the present, explain. He is willing to continue exploring and to learn what is there to be discovered by us all.

I have included a bit of biographical information because without it, my book would be a dry old story! I hope it will explain things to my children and grandchildren and to other friends and family. This book might also be interesting to those who have read my two yoga stories books and might be wondering about Guptananda.

I have a number of friends who are like-minded, and who are healers, writers, Reiki practitioners, crystal healers or mediums. They tend to just accept that everyone involved in these fields of interest has a similar understanding of what the 'Universe' is about, in as much as it can be understood by human minds. They tend not to talk about how their understanding came to be. I would be fascinated to know how it all dawned upon them, but life is busy, and there isn't time to recall all the incidents that occurred in normal conversations. Many of my friends were aware of their psychic abilities when they were very young, and they took it all for granted. It was not so for me. My father did have some belief in 'other forces', but when, at five years old, I told him how I was playing with the fairies, he said I mustn't do it. It was probably very wise in the circumstances, and as my father's word was law in our house, I stopped and shut off my psychic mind. You will have noticed that I considered only a few of the incidents which happened to me to be 'absolute proof'. The other events were indications, or interesting happenings to be noted and remembered. Confirmed sceptics would soon find reasons not to believe that what happened was numinous, or what some people might call paranormal. I used to be one of those sceptics.

If you have enjoyed this book you may want to go on to read my yoga stories books, if you haven't already. My next book will be about some of the traditions the First Nation people in America, who have been referred to as Native Americans or American Indians. As described in an earlier chapter, an indigenous Native American Chief spirit guide named Calling Horse gave me his stories, and it is high time they were published in an accessible format.

I would encourage everyone to open themselves to the spiritual side of their nature. This is best done under wise human guidance, however, where love, kindness and compassion are of crucial importance. We all have our guides and angels and they love to help us I am told, but of course I have no proof of that for anyone other than myself!

If you feel inclined to investigate a spiritual path for yourself, you need to keep asking and exploring. Find teachers that you can trust and who are trusted by other people you know. There are plenty of charlatans out there, just interested in your money. A genuine path will not be expensive to follow; true wisdom is often freely given. There is an Indian guru online at the moment, Sadguru, who is very popular. I find him quite obscure at times, but I heard him say that you will not find the truth unless you really want it so much that you weep for it. I do remember weeping and praying for clarity. Whether this really is a prerequisite, I don't know. It has been half a lifetime's work for me, but so very worthwhile.

~ PART 2 ~

A Background to My Childhood

Putting this book into perspective

My intention for writing this book was to describe the inexplicable events and happenings by 'normal scientific standards', which I experienced and that led me to believe in things beyond this world. I could not justify putting this **Part 2** section in the main body of the book as it is more 'normal' than 'mystical', but I have been told that it does need to feature, so here it is. For my family, those lovely boys I grew up with, for my own boys and for my nieces, nephews and grandchildren, here is a little bit more background. Other readers may be interested, especially if they feel a lack of spiritual connection in their lives, and wonder if they need to have been born with it, or can access it later in life, like me.

My Polish father – from 'hero to zero' and back again.

My dad's ambition after the war was to be a farmer. As a professional soldier, promoted to Lieutenant Colonel at the end of the war, his family was in business in Poland, and he had no farming background. He thought he could rely on his strong intellect and willingness to learn from books to make a go of it.

Dad and my Scottish mother had partnered with a Polish couple to buy a farm in Devon. Both couples used up all their savings, but the other couple wanted out after three years of farm life. It had not been a happy experience for them. Dad had to pay them back their deposit and, to find this money, he had to sell his milking herd. This left the farm with very little money – no milk cheque coming in. It was a bitter blow to my father and the following seven years were a very hard grind for my parents. At this point I arrived, their second child, a year and eight months after their first-born son, R, and followed three years later by my second brother, P.

Strangely enough, my first memory was of a spiritual event – my baptism. I was about three and a half, maybe nearer four years old and my parents had decided to have me baptised into the Catholic Church along with my new baby brother. I strongly resisted this, refusing to be held, screaming the church down. I was terrified. My father had told me that it was an important thing to do because then I would be able to go to heaven. Of course, as a small child I had no intentions of 'going to heaven'. I wanted to stay on earth and live forever, and that was that. Perhaps I thought that I had done enough screaming and crying to stop the procedure, and I thought I had escaped death. However when I was eight years old and in the class of a teacher I adored, Mr Goodwin, he dealt a bitter blow.

He told us, "Of course we all die, everyone has to die…"

I was distraught, how could my beloved teacher be so cruel? I had a fear of death which then lasted until my revelations at forty three years old. This manifested itself as a fear of funerals. At the first one I attended, I cried uncontrollably throughout the service, although I had never even met the deceased young man, and at the second funeral, for an uncle of my husband whom I had met only once, I was embarrassed to find myself sobbing. Tears for my late mother-in-law seemed more fitting, but at the time I seemed to be more affected than the rest of the family, who certainly loved her at least as much as I did, and probably a lot more, being her true offspring. Glad to say I'm not afflicted in that way any more!

We left the farm and moved to Ipswich when I was seven years old. Dad was offered training in an agricultural engineering company in order to become a European sales representative. Polish people are often good linguists, and my dad spoke Russian, German and French in addition to English and Polish. (He later added Spanish, Dutch and a good smattering of Italian.) A local magistrate, a very well-connected gentleman, whose daughter had married an officer in the Polish army, helped Dad to secure this post, having heard about my father's situation, and his struggles to make ends meet on the farm.

We three children were perfectly happy on the farm. We had everything we needed plus fields, woods and streams to play in. It was an idyllic life for kids. When my elder brother went to school, my younger brother was only two and stayed indoors with Mother. I played alone for two years. That's when the fairies came along and made me happy. They filled my days, and on occasion I felt the most delicious, exciting sensations when I was with them. I still wonder whether other girls experienced orgasms at that age and whether they, like me, thought that fairies were involved. But being somewhat shy about such things, I've never asked anyone else about it. I did tell my dad, no wonder he told me so severely not to play with the fairies!

At five years old I too trudged up the farm lane to catch the bus for my first day at school. I remember well the feeling of being in a box, totally contained, not able to escape. Come to think of it that must have been my first 'vision', an encapsulation of a strong feeling in a pictorial form. I had lost the freedom of the farm fields, woods and fairy friends and exchanged them for rows of desks and untrustworthy children. Somebody stole my precious new pencil box on the very first day and I knew who it was, but it seemed that nothing could be done about it. Luckily, I had a very nice teacher who guided me through those difficult first days of school although she could not retrieve my pencil box…

The stories that were read to us were very frightening to me. I didn't want to hear about giants at the tops of beanstalks, who could climb down and wallop you. I had to be rescued by the classroom assistant, who washed away my tears and told me that they were just a fairy stories and not to be frightened. I must have toughened up quite quickly. I got used to the 'box', the containment of school. I learned to read – something that had seemed daunting and impossible to me at first – and soon moved up out of the 'babies' class, as they called it.

On my first nature walk, maybe the only one we ever did, we were shown lamb's tails, or hazel catkins, and the teacher showed us the tiny little red hairs that would become the hazelnuts. I was fascinated. I loved plants and flowers, trees and mosses. They formed a very important part of my early life because we didn't have many toys to play with as such, but we could play with pebbles in the stream, tadpoles and frogs, slippery green algae in a chipped white enamel bowl, with the odd newt if I was very lucky. All these things kept us happy. We lived too far away from the village to have friends coming over to play and we had no car, but my mother had managed to find herself some bridge buddies – a fact that I was unaware of until she came to live with us at the very end of her life.

"Surely you remember the Robsons," she said, "we visited them once; they had a farm."

I did remember visiting them. They were so sweet and kind, younger than my parents, childless and naïve. They suggested my brother and I went upstairs to see their glass animals.

"Mind the hole in the floor on the landing," they said, not realising that we were far more of a danger to the glass animals than the hole in the floor was to us. Up we went. We carefully traversed the large hole in the floorboards and entered their very sparse bedroom. Ranged along the window ledge was a collection of tiny delicate glass animals each one half the size of my little hand. We picked them up and looked at them. I swear that's all we did. Just looked at them. But one by one they all broke. Delicate little legs and horns just seemed to fall off. I might have been three or four and my brother a couple of years older. Old enough to know we were in trouble and old enough to know not to mention it – ever. At the age of fifty-one, I confessed all to my mum. She gave a wry smile and said, "Oh dear, I did wonder why they never invited us back!"

We moved to Ipswich, spending one night at an aunt's house in London on the way. There were electric light switches everywhere, a light in every room! We were mesmerised. My elder brother just had to keep switching them on and off. On the farm the paraffin lamps would occasionally burst into flames and have to be carried hastily outdoors. They were our only experience of sources of light. In the mid-1950s that's how rural life was.

Our new primary school in Ipswich seemed huge. There were two classes in every year group. I sat next to a badly behaved smelly, snotty boy. I asked the teacher to move me.

We were country bumpkins, but clever enough. My big brother R was bullied because of his unusual accent, so I decided I would try to speak like the locals. I used to practise saying 'good noight', and 'switch on the loight', Ipswich style. I soon made friends. What a treat it was to be able to pop round to my friend's house just down the road from us.

A third brother arrived in my family when I was nine. After his birth, my mother was able to smile again. The pregnancy took its toll on Mum, at forty and with three other children to look after, she always seemed worn out. But my little brother brought the sunshine into our lives again. I gave up my dolls now I had a real live baby to play with, cuddle and look after. I so enjoyed my little brother S, he was a contented and cheerful baby. I could take him out in his pram and show him off to the neighbours. My brother P was also a jolly chap. He had snowy white-blond hair, apple cheeks and the most winning smile. He was really a very pretty child, people used to say he was so pretty that he should have been a girl.

One day my friend and I persuaded P to dress up as a girl. We put a headscarf on him to hide his short hair, his glorious snowy fringe added to his appeal, a touch of Mum's lipstick and he was ready for the promenade. We took S out in his pram. P walked alongside, and we introduced him as our American cousin, Susan, to anyone who was interested enough to stop and talk. They played along with us. P put on his best American accent, which for a child of seven was easy enough to do, or so we thought. Such hilarity.

P always saw the funny side of things, he was a terrible tease but we couldn't help laughing. He used to capture me on the stairs on my way to the bathroom, and refuse to let me go – when that's exactly what I needed to do. It was excruciating! But he'd be giggling away and pretending that nothing was wrong and I didn't know whether to laugh or scream, and I usually did both.

My youngest brother S had lots of friends. Mum was very good at welcoming all-comers. My friends and the boys' friends would often stay to tea. We had to pull the dining room table out from the wall for every meal, the rooms in our semi-detached house were so small, but it mattered not, there was always space for an extra child or two.

My brothers did exciting things like going fishing, sailing and canoeing. Somehow those kinds of activity passed me by, maybe because girls just didn't do that sort of thing in my day. Or perhaps because my brothers' friends did. My eldest brother R made his own canvas canoe, constructed a trailer for it and pulled it around on his pushbike. I was very impressed at the time and, looking back, that was some achievement! He did become an engineer.

I did feel an inner longing for more excitement in my life. Sewing my own clothes, knitting, and cooking didn't quite cut it. Luckily the swimming club, which we attended weekly for many years, and the Girls' Venture Corps, which I joined at thirteen, provided a different sort of attraction, namely boys…

One of the boys had a copy of '*Lady Chatterley's Lover*', a book that had been banned after it was written, in the 1920s, but then allowed on to the market in the 1960s. The naughty pages were well thumbed – they were a revelation to me. I had no idea that sex could sound so simple, natural and appealing! Compared to today's overt sexuality, it was milk and water. The book didn't make me want to experiment though. Even then I didn't understand the fuss. Why ban the book? This was before the days of the pill and 'free love', which came just three or four years later. Careless sex often resulted in pregnancy and the terrible choices of abortion or adoption, or keeping a baby in usually very difficult circumstances. I was almost innocent of all this, but it lurked at the back of my mind, because a girl from school was 'sent away'. I might have mentioned it to Mum, but it was not something I talked about openly at home, because I thought it might send my dad into a fury, and he would forbid me from going out.

We had a huge, old black Humber Super Snipe – of the sort used in funerals to carry the mourners

– large enough to carry our family of six plus a couple of friends sometimes. Mum and Dad used to take us on 'outings' every so often. There were many pretty picnic spots by the River Orwell and the River Deben, only a few miles away. Dad would play army games with us, pretending to be sneaking up on the enemy; we would crawl on our bellies and hide behind bushes, until the one who was the catcher saw us. We had barbeques on the heath as a special treat. The beach was also an ideal place to practise yoga with Dad – he was a great believer in it. We would do balancing acts and hone our yoga poses. Meanwhile Mum would be doing *The Telegraph* crossword – she didn't indulge in 'horse play' as she might have called it – when our human pyramid toppled to the ground! Mother preferred teaching her Scottish country dancing class to rough and tumble with a bit of yoga thrown in.

We were a noisy, quarrelsome bunch at times, especially on car journeys. After a few years Dad left Mum to do the weekend trips out. He preferred to enjoy a day of peace at his allotments, while we went out on our picnics on the coast or by the river. We felt more relaxed when Dad was not driving. He had a quick temper, and being 'the old colonel', he expected obedience from his troops, and when he didn't get it, we would feel his wrath. He never actually hit me, but his anger was enough to make me stop whatever it was that was happening in the back of the car, if I could! I'm not sure if he ever hit the boys – he certainly threatened to.

Those days of trips to the seaside were filled with fun and joy. In spring and summer Mum saw it as her happy duty to take us out at the weekends to nice places where we could play and explore in the wild. She made superb picnics, or at the very least, if it was just an afternoon out (perhaps for a dip in the sea at Felixstowe) there would be a 'shivery bite' – a packet or two of biscuits. This was in the days when only Digestives or Rich Tea were available.

After S grew beyond the baby and toddler stage, I didn't play with him so much, but we were always close. I was becoming a horrible teenager with ambitions above my station. At thirteen I wanted to distance myself from all our parents' social activities. Occasionally I would go along to Mums Scottish Dance Society. The dancing was very mentally demanding and seemed really complicated to me. It gave me no pleasure to be hurled around by great big men with beards, swirling kilts and sporrans. The Scottish Dancing Society held a Christmas party for families. I was disdainful. I didn't want to be associated with little kids rushing around, dragging each other along the floor, or with those huge and hairy men with big smiles and big knees. I went on strike. Mum got the message. She was pretty disappointed and embarrassed by my sulky face. Sorry Mum!

At fourteen I was allowed to have boyfriends but, fortunately, the effect of the church's teachings made me very wary of boys, once I had managed to attract them into asking me out. Kissing was great fun with some boys, but most hadn't got a clue! Anything else was strictly not allowed by me. I made it clear what I wanted, and it didn't include any fumbling hands caressing my body. My mother said I was boy mad. I had so many boyfriends, but none of them lasted more than a day or two or beyond a couple of weeks of knowing them. My dad was my example of an ideal man – clever, confident, dignified, handsome and amusing. He was my hero. In comparison my boyfriends were mostly very disappointing. Looking back I now realise that my parents might have completely misunderstood my very frequent changes of boyfriend. It was because I didn't want to give them what they wanted – not because I was some kind of teenage nymphomaniac!

Very soon after my fourteenth birthday my adoration for my dad turned into resentment, because he seemed reluctant to allow me to do what I wanted to do – things that were officially agreed with Mum, I was now allowed to wear make up and go out with boys! He just didn't trust boys, but he would never tell me why and I didn't understand what his problem was. He never explained about devious men getting girls drunk, date rape, or anything of that sort. He just became bad-tempered and our closeness evaporated. I wish he had explained those things to me because when I left home, along came the sharks, and I didn't even see them coming.

Dad's mistrust of boys was complicated by a strange occurrence that happened on my first night out at a party. My parents told me to be home by nine-thirty, and I returned home, oblivious to the time, at eleven. Dad was cross, furious even. I was puzzled. My watch said nine-thirty; it had genuinely stopped. I was not a liar, that is what happened, but perhaps at the time my dad, who didn't trust boys was wondering if he could now trust me. As far as I could tell, he did not question my brothers about what they were doing– it seemed like I alone was the problem, probably because I was a 'vulnerable' female, and didn't realise what that vulnerability was, because no one really explained. I was no more vulnerable than any other girl of my age.

I was fortunate to find a Catholic boy, an altar boy, no less, who had the same attitudes as I did regarding sex. In addition he seemed to be all the things my father was. Mature, (two years older than me), very clever and handsome, confident and charming – and joy of joys – he had a sports car! We were far too young to be 'serious' and we had an on and off relationship for three years, before he went off to medical school. My parents liked him. I adored him, but even he had feet of clay and dumped me for another girl just before leaving for university. That was my first experience of being rejected, and very painful it was too. No doubt at that age it was the best thing for us both. He came back into my life online very briefly, via Friends Reunited, and I was able to learn about his life, his fame as an obstetrician, his divorce, remarriage and life of luxury in a tax haven. That wouldn't have suited me at all, being a country girl at heart, in love with my plants and animals, and later enjoying my spiritual life. However, it was a great pick-me-up to know that he had valued me enough to seek me out at the age of fifty-eight, and at a time when my life was quite sad and difficult. I was able to let him go with no regrets or recriminations at all, after that gulf of forty-five years.

I don't know how our dear mum kept up with all of us kids. Being quite wide apart in age, we had different needs. Dad was working abroad half the time, (after I was about ten years old) in Germany, France, Spain and much of the rest of Europe too. He sold agricultural equipment. So it was left to Mother to ferry us round, clothe us (she made our clothes whenever possible), feed us and keep the house clean. In the holidays for many years we kids would go bean picking most days to earn some pocket money. We cycled three miles to the bean fields. I loved those summers, it gave me a sense of personal power and responsibility to earn some cash in return for a bit of hard work. It was fun, too, being there with my friends and my brothers. When I was old enough I took a summer job in a department store in the fashion boutique. How I loved that job! I hadn't a clue about clothes as all mine were homemade, but the staff (another girl and I) were allowed to choose what we wanted to wear from the stock while we were on duty. What a bonus!

In term times I was so taken up with my school life and youth club nights, that I hardly noticed what my brothers were doing, but I do know that cubs and sea-scouts were part of their picture. We lived twelve miles from the sea, but had a number of rivers and estuaries nearby. S has had many different canoes in his life, sometimes several at once, each for a different purpose. He lived in Wellington, New Zealand for thirty years – plenty of scope for seafaring there! P loved windsurfing and sailing on lakes where he lived in France, and R takes his family out in canoes and on his motorboat in Australia where he has lived all his adult life. Mother always said she loved the water, and it seems the boys all loved it too.

The three eldest in my family all went to university. My parents were very proud of us. In those days we got grants that paid for everything. Mother went back to teaching at the local secondary modern school. S, being six years younger than P, was alone at home as, one by one, we all left. He felt a great pressure from our parents to go to university like the rest of us, but he really did not want to go. He wanted to become a carpenter. He was skilled with his hands, but also cleverer than all of us, I always thought. He thought my parents just loved to boast about their children all going to university, and said that was their motive for wanting him to go. It was not a very common thing in those days, to have a university education. I'm not sure S was right. It's true they couldn't resist a bit of boasting, but they also saw how clever and capable he was. They really wanted him to get the most from his life, which in their opinion should be accessed via a degree.

My dad was sixty-six when these decisions were made. S had spent his teenage years with a dad aged over sixty, whose patience and understanding had worn thin. The atmosphere between them was not good at all. S left home at eighteen and became a canoeing instructor in Wales. His path to a career that used his talents and abilities eventually took him to the National Museum in Wellington, New Zealand, where they relied on him for the many practical tasks that running a museum and creating displays involves. He was always very practical, able to teach himself whatever skills he needed to know. S, a keen bird watcher, enjoyed sea kayaking for many years and used his skills to study, visit and protect penguins in their nesting boxes. These he made and placed in suitable locations around the coast, to encourage penguins to breed away from people and marauding dogs. S is now enjoying a new and very different chapter in his life.

R went to Australia and worked on various marine engineering projects, married an Australian girl, had two Aussie daughters and never looked back. The fact that all my brothers left England in their early twenties might have had something to do with needing to put a big distance between themselves and our parents because of my Dad's dominating nature. I used to wonder about that. Or maybe because Dad was an 'alien' and did not have strong ties with the UK, his attitude transferred itself to them. The boys all returned home quite regularly to the UK, and all was sweetness and light in their adult years with regard to our parents. P's visits were sadly curtailed by his illness and premature death.

The only mystical event that I was aware of in my childhood, were the ones involving the fairies and the Ouija board when I was fourteen. Like me, many have lived to regret such experiments. However My dad had some mystical leanings. He prided himself on being a wart charmer! This was a useful skill for farmers, because cows' udders sometimes get warty, and it makes for uncomfortable hand milking, both for the milker and the poor cow. It was the only way of milking on small farms in those days. He also charmed human warts. I was fascinated to hear about our family doctor in Ipswich, who had a very warty young son, whose warts clung to him stubbornly. His father could not get rid of them, so my dad offered to charm them, and did so successfully. He wouldn't tell me how to do it, and when I became a healer I asked him about it again. He said he couldn't really translate the Polish words that he used for wart-charming, so I never did learn the skill. The fact that they disappeared from cattle puts paid to the idea that wart charming acts through the patient's psyche.

In my forties, Dad was pleased that I had become a healer and let me know that he believed in 'energy' and that it could be used for good or ill. He had read books about the subject and experimented on one occasion, not with giving energy to another person, but taking it. He regretted what he did, however, and never repeated it. He explained that he was at a very low, exhausted and lonely point in his travels in Europe, and he decided to see if he could boost his energy by getting into someone's aura, and taking energy, using a method he had read about but didn't believe. He was on a crowded bus standing next to a young woman. She seemed to be full of life and health, and after a while she began to droop and to look confused, she staggered off the bus he was travelling on, and it seemed clear to him that he felt better while she looked drained. It troubled him and he told me he vowed never to do it again. He always wanted to do 'the right thing', but on this occasion he slipped up. The Christian approach on this would be *'do as you would be done by'* meaning *treat others the way we want them to treat us*, and the Hindu law of karma says *'what you send out, you get back'*.

Mother was an atheist and had no time for religion, but she did not approve or disapprove of our church-going activities. They gave her a free Sunday morning, and maybe that's exactly what she and Dad needed. She had married a Catholic and went along with what was expected in those days: that any child from the marriage must be brought up a Catholic.

My idea to start practising yoga after the birth of my first child was certainly seeded by my dad. He practised yoga virtually every day of his adult life. In the mornings before the rest of the family got up he would spend twenty minutes doing his stretches. And after lunch he would always take a twenty-minute nap. He never called it meditation but it probably had the same effect. He was always full of energy; his career in the Polish army had started as a PE instructor. Perhaps yoga came to Poland before it hit our shores in the fifties? He continued to practise till the age of eighty-seven when he passed away.

He had redeemed himself to me and became my hero again after those turbulent teenage years. If you're listening, thanks for everything, Dad, not forgetting those super-duper German roller skates, with extra-strong fibreglass wheels – the best present I ever had!

I had a good childhood with a few ups and downs, but mostly very happy memories for which I am grateful.

I never thought that I would be writing books in my retirement, I only ever received a B++ at best for my essays at school, an A was beyond my reach. I wonder what I'll get for this effort. Another B++ perhaps, but at least I have told my story and it isn't quite run of the mill is it?

~ APPENDIX 1 ~

The subtle energy system

When you get into the healing world, you discover an aspect of being human that neither orthodox medicine nor organised religion in the Christian West seem to have recognised.

The subtle energy system – the auras, the chakras and meridians – is understood by both Chinese medicine and also by followers of the Eastern religions, such as Hinduism and Buddhism. When we are first introduced to the idea of subtle energy we need to remain open-minded and see it as one of those 'possibilities of things that might be true', until we come to discover that it is real. The chakras can be felt in one's hands once one becomes attuned to them. They can also be seen as points or patches of light. Anyone who wishes to observe chakras needs to be in an appropriate state of being, with their own energies open and balanced, before they can see or feel such energies in others.

The chakras represent, affect and are affected by every aspect of what it is to be human. Chakras, or energy centres, can be broadly categorised: there are seven main ones and many more subsidiaries. It would take a whole book to describe them, as

Barbara Anne Brennan has done in *Hands of Light*. A number of other authors have also produced work on the chakras.

I will condense the knowledge by giving a bare-bones analysis of the purpose and function of the chakras.

The first, or base, chakra, is at the lower end of the spine in the coccygeal region.
It is about the amount of physical energy and connection to the Earth, or 'grounded-ness', we have. Survival instincts, survival of the species and therefore reproduction and the health and growth of your bones, are controlled by this chakra.

The second chakra is in the lower belly and deals with the emotional and physical aspects of sex and reproduction together with joy and creativity, including artistic creativity of every sort.

The third chakra is at the solar plexus. It deals with the power or energy distribution of the body and also personal power, memory and the physical organs in that area.

The fourth chakra is the heart centre and is concerned with our heartfelt or loving connection with our families, friends, humanity, the natural world, and (if we have one) our deity. It deals with all aspects of love and governs the circulatory system, lungs and other organs in the vicinity.

The fifth chakra is the throat centre, which deals with self-expression and communication and, as with all chakras, it governs all organs in that area of the body.

The sixth centre is the third eye. It is situated in the middle of the forehead. It is the control centre for all the other chakras and also deals with intuition and higher creative and perceptive abilities, such as clairaudience and clairvoyance.

The crown chakra, at the top of the head, is the seat of the soul. It is believed that this chakra houses the part of the individual that is Divine and immortal. Spiritual happenings occur via the crown chakra, and one can feel it becoming active – almost tingling – when opening up to meditate or to give healing.

The chakras can exist in different states of openness (positivity), or may be closed, indicating an unwillingness to engage, or even spin backwards (indicating negativity), when the world is perceived as a dangerous place and interaction is avoided at the particular level of the negative chakra. For example, in those experiencing sexual abuse, the second or sacral chakra may become closed, or negative, and the victim may not be able or willing subsequently to engage in normal healthy, loving sexual activity. We are taught that this can be corrected with appropriate help.

Another example of reduced activity or closure

of a specific chakra is, if as a child, our voice or opinion has often been ridiculed or suppressed, we may find our throat chakra is rather inactive, and we are frustrated by not being able to freely express ourselves in speech. Again, with help this can be remedied.

There are a number of methods of dealing with such traumas, and wise advice can lead to various solutions, through psychological counselling, spiritual healing and other appropriate modalities.

~ APPENDIX 2 ~

The workings of a pendulum

The pendulum can be used for many purposes, It can be used on maps to dowse for water or minerals, or to find lost items. It can be used over charts of numbers to identify numbered objects or places. Pendulum work is a study of its own. I have found it really useful for choosing remedies e.g. herbs, Bach Flowers and essential oils to treat specific problems. The fact that answers can be found in books makes it easy to check the choices that the pendulum makes. I feel remedies are very personal, and specific to the patient, so I want to find exactly the right oil for the job, for me, or the person I am treating.

I have a large collection of oils because my friend was selling them and I bought one a month until I had her whole collection! Each oil has a number of properties and many oils have similar uses. I could not possibly remember the properties of them all, hence the usefulness of the pendulum. Frequently I ask about suitable oils for a bath, to prepare myself for an event such as choir practice or giving a talk. I ask the pendulum to choose suitable oils to make me feel alert, relaxed, open and friendly. To give a talk I might ask to feel energised, confident, open, happy and able to concentrate. Over the years I have come to recognise the oils suitable for these functions, but I still prefer to dowse, as something might be needed that I haven't thought about.

I always choose essential oils rather than orthodox medicine if possible.

On the first occasion I was looking for a remedy using my pendulum, I was suffering from a particularly annoying personal condition, I dowsed to find the right oils. Lavender and myrrh came up. I then checked in my book and found the condition in the index. Lavender and myrrh were the preferred remedy. Very gratifying! This has happened so many times now that I know it works, for me at least. My pendulum has sixty different oils to choose from and each oil has a number allocated to it. The numbers chart consists of protractor-like shapes divided into 'cake sections', from one to ten, then eleven to twenty and so on – see the diagram. The details of how to use the chart will be found in any decent book on the use of the pendulum.

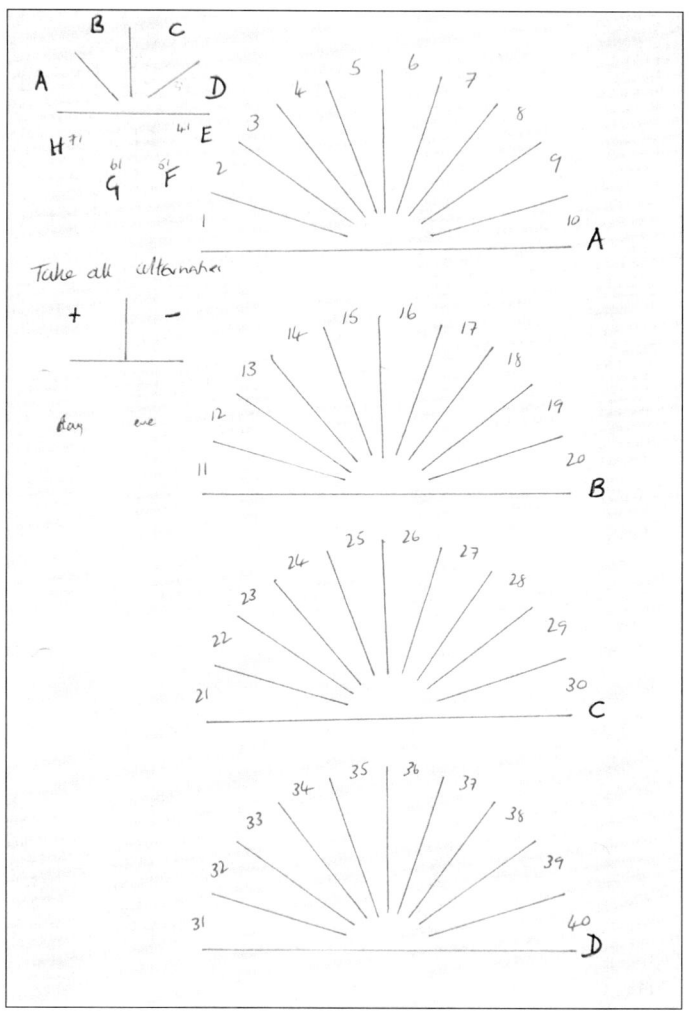

To me, this was another proof that there are energies that can be helpful to us but are not recognised by most scientists. People who dowse for water are universally recognised as having a useful skill, but nobody could tell you how it works. It is called water *divining*, and I think the god force, or Divinity, is involved in some inexplicable way. I believe the pendulum acts in the same way as the divining rods of the water diviner. With divining it is important not to have any opinions or desires about the outcome, because our minds can move the pendulum.

My husband Bryn was open to unexplained phenomena. In his time in the Navy he had watched UFOs dancing in the sky over the Atlantic Ocean. He had seen his long-deceased uncle apparently sitting in a sports car, of which he had several, and waving to Bryn as he drove by. When Bryn was visiting the poppy fields of Flanders, a spectral soldier's presence had shouted to him as it trudged along a path between two French villages. He was almost as keen as I was to try to prove that these mystical happenings were 'real'.

The workings of the pendulum intrigued both of us. They are notoriously tricky to use, but can give fascinating factual results when these are 'deemed to be appropriate'. Deemed by whom? Don't ask me! I just thank the 'Universe' for this kind of help, that leaves the methodology up for debate. I devised an experiment to try to prove to Bryn that the pendulum had some very interesting 'capabilities'. Bryn and I had very different views on what was good and healthy to eat. I am all for fresh food, vegetables, fruit and nuts and nothing processed if possible. Bryn liked sausages, bacon, processed peas, baked beans with perhaps a bit of a veg on the side, and if they were canned or frozen, no problem. In his life in the Navy, he had thrived on that kind of food for years and wouldn't fault it.

I dreamt up an experiment to see if the pendulum could tell us which out of three types of pea had the most 'life force', or prana, as yogis call it: I wanted it to show us which peas were the healthiest to eat. We had fresh peas growing on our allotment, some frozen peas in the freezer, and a can of marrowfat peas in the cupboard.

It had to be a blind test, where the peas were hidden under something, and I wanted the test to be repeated at least ten times. This we did. The peas sat in upturned jar lids, covered over by white china bowls. There were three positions marked on the table, one, two and three. One round of the test involved me holding the pendulum and asking which were the best peas. The pendulum would move towards the chosen pot. I would record the position of the pot and Bryn would record what was actually in the jar lid beneath the pot. I would then turn away and he would move the peas into a different position, and off we went again – where were the best peas now?

In every case the pendulum chose the fresh peas. Ten times out of ten. Magic or what?

I have tried to repeat this trial to no avail. It seems that whatever drives the pendulum does not 'want' to be tested for the sake of it. I believe there needs to be a good reason to test for particular answers. On that successful first occasion, ultimately, I was trying to get Bryn to improve his eating habits for the sake of his health, but I think the damage had already been done. He died at the age of sixty-four, a confirmed smoker and eater of sausages and bacon. Such a lovely husband, full of love, jokes and stories, sadly missed.

Details of my other books:

Book 1 **The Great Little Book of Yoga Stories**, *Yoga Philosophy for All*
This title is about the *Yamas* and *Niyamas*, or the rules of life, and it is for middle-grade readers, children from ten to thirteen, and yoga fans of all ages.
First published, 2019 by Sifi Publishing; re-published, 2022 by Top of the Village Publishing – topofthevillagepublishing.co.uk

Book 2 **Yoga Stories from Guru Guptananda**, *How to be Happy and Healthy – Yoga Wisdom Explained*
This title features stories about the Eight Limbs of Yoga and the Chakras, it is also for middle-grade readers and yoga fans of all ages.
First published, 2022, by Top of the Village Publishing – *topofthevillagepublishing.co.uk*

Audiobook: Yoga Stories from Guru Guptananda, read by Abhishek Morye,
published by Top of the Village Publishing, 2022

If you have enjoyed my book, please spread the word and leave a review on *topofthevillagepublishing,co.uk*, or my website: *yogastories.co.uk*. I feel very strongly that this information and help needs to get out into the world. It opens doors to so much more in life, and connects us to our Higher Selves and that which is Divine in every single human being. Who knows what help is out there for us all? Jesus, Buddha, Mohammed, Krishna and others are not in competition with each other, but via years of culture and tradition they work with those who are open to them. Many people have been turned off religion as such, but in my opinion we are all made up of body, mind and spirit, and that spirit part of us is the most durable, everlasting and most important part of our being. We need to nurture it and to learn what is needed to foster spiritual growth for ourselves and others in our lives.

This first limited edition of my book will act as a 'pilot' and will be sent to friends and relations, and feedback is very welcome so that I know if it worth publishing in the wider world. Please do contact me at tessa.hillman2@gmail.com with any comments, appreciative, puzzled or otherwise.

Acknowledgements

I have received help and encouragement from my editors who looked carefully through the book and suggested adjustments according to their own expertise and background.

My husband David Guiterman, Helen Greathead, Becky Pickard, Sarah Kearney, Emily Morley, Emily Ould, Julie Lloyd, Sandy Winterton, Jan Phillips, Angie Sage, Jenny Bourne, Fiona Prentice, Kim Chamberlain, Jenna Reece, Ruth Stead, Jill Wigley, Hilary Matthieu, Terri Nixon, Danielle Lowy and several others have all helped me in various ways to correct the fault lines in this book.

Thanks to Alan Nisbet for the cover picture and to Liz Hyde, graphic artist www.elizabethhydedesign.co.uk who worked on the final design of the cover.

I would also like to thank Patrick Gamble for his painting of the guru.

B.K.S Iyengar, through his book Light on Yoga, has been a very important source of information for me throughout my years as a yoga teacher. I would like to express my appreciation of his work.

This book would not have been published if it were not for the help of the above people, but it would never have happened at all if it were not for

Swami Ramesh Guptananda coming into my mind and giving me the Yoga Stories, for which I am eternally grateful. Also those in spirit who have added hugely to my appreciation of spiritual matters and to my understanding that other realms exist and are inextricably connected with our own Earth realm, thank you all!